"A principal figure in the sub-field of Africana Women's Studies, Clenora has received national & international attention. This book—an empowering overview of her paradigm, considered by many a global signature concept on the subject—continues her solid scholarly record of crafting means by which we can better secure true social justice. Congratulations on another milestone!"

James B. Stewart, PhD, Inaugural Dir. of BERC-21, Senior Fellow at the Institute on Race, Power & Political Economy, The New School (NYC); Professor Emeritus & Vice Provost, Penn State U.

“*Elevating Humanity via Africana Womanism* gives us a greater sense of what has been missing and what is still needed to bring wholeness, peace and justice for all humankind. Having identified the key unaddressed issues, often buried in hidden truths, Clenora, then, offers a corrective, thereby making progress via conceivable possibilities for ending the race divide within the human race.”

Gail Baker, PhD, Senior Vice President & Provost; Interim Dean, School of Peace Studies, U of San Diego

“Dr. Hudson (Weems) continues to encapsulate the importance of community, synergy & collaboration within the Black family. As an aspiring 3rd generation Black physician (my father is a gastroenterologist; grandfather was a urologist), with an ambition to learn, serve, progress & elevate our communities, I, too, practice Africana Womanism’s family centrality, epitomized in its mandate for Collectivity for social justice.”

Benjamin Jones, MD Candidate Class of **2025**, U of KS School of Medicine; my former student and an Africana Womanism mentee

“Guided by Dr. Clenora Hudson (Weems), Africana Womanism continues to ‘elevate humanity,’ shining indelible light in a cloudy landscape of yesterday and today. In embracing her insights for ending social injustices, we, then, would be that collective force needed to end inequities at last.”

Alveda C. King, PhD, Evangelist; Niece of Dr. Martin Luther King, Jr.; Founder: speakforlife.org and Leader of Civil Rights for the Unborn

“Africana Womanism elevates humanity by building a sense of community like *Ubuntu*. Through the ethics of caring & solidarity, our humanity carries the sense of justice from one to another among Africana men, women, & children. All lives are fulfilled when Africana people are fulfilled. Africana Womanism elevates its community through loving ourselves, our neighbor, & nature. It moves the world & the individual in every family to live in love & shared experiences. Africana Womanism is the act of witnessing the worth of those who came before us ; & are still among us.”

Suzete de Paiva Lima Kourliansdsky, *Mahura* Collective—*Paris*, France

“Dr. Clenora Hudson (Weems) has once again broken new ground. This massive, little book is an indispensable resource for those wanting a theoretical framework that eschews division and, instead, embraces unity in the Black

Family, and beyond. To be sure, a global concept, with conceivable workable solutions, it merits the status of being required reading for all humanity."

Pamela Reed, PhD, Professor & Founding Executive Director, James Arthur Baldwin Africologic Institute, Virginia State U; Interview, with Clenora Hudson, *Prologue*, *Africana Womanism* 6th Edition

"The Africana Womanism paradigm justifiably centers the Africana woman in her community, via establishing a learning objective that can eradicate white supremacy. The author elucidates a smooth & awe-inspiring claim that if we seek justice for the most vulnerable & mistreated, it could result in an overdue snowball of global justice, thereby, advancing the condition for all humanity."

Jacqueline Roebuck Sakho, PhD, Assistant Professor, Leadership Studies, North Carolina A & T State U

"*Elevating Humanity via Africana Womanism*, a wholesome book that reaches readers inside & outside academia, offers Africana people the reflection needed to improve our living conditions. It guides us through a family-centered dynamics to help harmonize the roles of our women & men in nurturing our children through a pathway of a new paradigm, finally detached from the misguided ideas that were the basis of the exploitation of global melanated people for centuries."

Helen Santos, Afro-Latina linguist in *US*—translator for Mulherismo Africana group—currently working with communities, emancipatory perspective of language acquisition

"Intra-connecting Africana Womanism and Healing Our Youth—Dr. Clenora Hudson (Weems) has introduced an authentic blueprint for the community to reconnect with God, demystify Eurocentric behaviors, and reclaim our love for one another—men, women & children. Our youth are in dire need of being replenished and involved in the process of collectively healing their wounds as they are guided by the principles of Africana Womanism."

Denisha Seals, Artist, filmmaker & author of Children's books (i.e., *The Butterflies in Me*)

"Clenora's theory expounds on the importance of sticking together for true security and success. The beauty of it all is the inclusivity of its participants and its audience—men, women and children, of all ages. Let's step it up, while beautifully embracing each other to make it happen for us all!"

Lillian A. Smith, Entrepreneur, former Senior Producer of the *Phil Donahue Show*, and former Executive Producer for *Fox TV in LA*

Elevating Humanity via Africana Womanism

Elevating Humanity via Africana Womanism is a short but powerful book, advocating synergy via unity/collectivity as a panacea for all societal ills. It discusses the theory of Africana Womanism—an authentic family centrality concept for all women of African descent—as a grid upon which to erect the private and public personae of all positive Africana people. Within the context of our cultural and historical matrix, it opens with defining the paradigm, while promoting the importance of prioritizing race, class, and gender, the triple plight of Black women. A workable strategy for ensuring equality for all, it closes on a note of love and spirituality, while embracing the special connection between Africana men and women, indeed, the two-sided human coin.

This introduction logically and convincingly speaks truth to power about who we, Black women, are, beginning, in Part I, with naming and defining ourselves, with the foreknowledge of the seminal role of our male counterparts. It identifies the 18 descriptors of the true Africana woman and her male counterpart. Part II offers a fruitful commentary, by sharing some of the many contributions we have given to society, which could enhance self-esteem among our people, many of whom have come to not love themselves and even their own, due to inadequate historical documentation.

Clenora Hudson (Weems) is a Professor, Theorist, Film Writer, and an Honored Listee in *Marquis Who's Who* 2024. She is the author of six books on Africana Women and four on Emmett Till, having established him as catalyst of the Civil Rights Movement in her 1988 dissertation. She is editor of *Africana-Melanated Womanism: In It Together* (2002); *Africana Paradigms, Practices & Literary Texts: Evoking Social Justice* (2021); *Physical and Intellectual Lynchings: An Emmett Till Continuum* (2007); and *Contemporary Africana Theory, Thought & Action: A Guide to Africana Studies* (2007). She is the recipient of the Ford and National Endowment for the Humanities Fellowships and, with her co-author, the 1998 Toni Morrison Society National Book Award. She was an Ida Beam Distinguished V. Professor, U of Iowa, AAS, delivering the Keynote Address "*Nobel Laureate Toni Morrison as Model Africana Womanist Artivist for Social Justice*," for its 50th anniversary.

Routledge Focus on Literature

Colonial Philippines in Italian Travel Writing
"Italians" Interpreting Difference
Jillian Loise Melchor

Essays on The Glass Menagerie
Truth in the Pleasant Disguise of Illusion
Tania Chakravertty

Margaret Wise Brown's Experimental Art
The Modernist Picture Book
Julia Pond

Tolkien and the Kalevala
Jyrki Korpua

Elevating Humanity via Africana Womanism
Clenora Hudson (Weems)

Reading Modernity, Modernism and Religion Today
Spinoza and Van Gogh
Patrick Grant

The Sagas of Icelanders
An Introduction to All Forty Sagas with Summaries
Annette Lassen

For more information about this series, please visit: www.routledge.com/Routledge-Focus-on-Literature/book-series/RFLT

Elevating Humanity via Africana Womanism

Clenora Hudson (Weems)

NEW YORK AND LONDON

First published 2025
by Routledge
605 Third Avenue, New York, NY 10158

and by Routledge
4 Park Square, Milton Park, Abingdon, Oxon, OX14 4RN

Routledge is an imprint of the Taylor & Francis Group, an informa business

ISBN: 9781032720012 (hbk)
ISBN: 9781032720043 (pbk)
ISBN: 9781032720036 (ebk)

DOI: 10.4324/9781032720036

Typeset in Times New Roman
by codeMantra

To my mom, Mary Cohran Pearson (1924–2018)—my Model Africana Womanist—family, and friends

I dedicate this book to all of us in celebration of all—men, women, and children—who commit ourselves to a unified struggle. Africana people must have a commitment and responsibility to each other so that the rich legacy of true Africana womanhood, for the survival of our entire family as collective warriors in the battle for our birthright as determiners of our fate and freedom, can live on. "To God Be the Glory."

In memory of 14-year-old Emmett Louis "Bobo" Till (1941–1955), whose August 28 1955 brutal lynching was the true catalyst of the Civil Rights Movement, established in "Emmett Louis Till: The Impetus of the Modern Civil Rights Movement," the 1988 Ford Doctoral Dissertation (U of Iowa), published in 1994 as *Emmett Till: The Sacrificial Lamb of the Civil Rights Movement)*. Emmett, a male, is the flip side of the human coin and must be likewise treated with equal respect. We're family!

Contents

Foreword

Marquita Gammage, PhD, Professor and Chair, Africana Studies Department, California State University, Northridge

> The first African American woman intellectual to formulate a position on Africana Womanism was Clenora Hudson (Weems), author of the 1993 groundbreaking study, *Africana Womanism: Reclaiming Ourselves*. Taking a strong position that black women should not pattern their liberation after Eurocentric feminism but after the historic and triumphant women of African descent, Hudson (Weems) has launched a new critical discourse in the Black Women's Literary Movement.
>
> *(Liggins Hill, Call and Response 1811)*

The sculpting of an ideology of existence and resistance for Africana women from their own cultural truths gave birth to a movement, *Africana Womanism*, that transformed our engagement with Africana women and their communities globally. In her unprecedented work, *Africana Womanism: Reclaiming Ourselves*, Clenora Hudson (Weems) weaves together the philosophies of Africana women, such as Sojourner Truth, to reposition the framing of Black womanhood away from a feminist agenda, which is inherently wedded to mainstream patriarchy, into a culturally literate paradigm, designed to embolden and empower Black women to interrogate the systems that impact their lives from an Afrocentric framework.

Dr. Clenora Hudson (Weems) empathizes with the Africanness of her own—Black people, Black cultures, and Black liberation—which transports us away from universal theories. In particular, the reclamation of self, through self-naming and self-definition, signified an important departure from the dominant narrative of feminism, and awakened a revival of African cultural heritage, philosophy, and perspectives for Africana women. This shift was not simply symbolic or surface level. Diverging from the Eurocentric paradigm of gender—represented in an authentic non-Western terminology and its definition, which specifies the prioritization of race, class, and gender in a family-centered theoretical construct—meant abandoning first the name itself, feminism, for Black women, which encompasses the social and political constructs that confined Black women to a marginal existence that operated only by extension of and/or in comparison to whiteness and white femininity. Hudson (Weems) clarifies this point, as she perceptively asserts that

> …Placing all women's history under White women's history, thereby giving the latter the definitive position, is problematic. In fact, it demonstrates the ultimate of racist arrogance and domination, suggesting that authentic activity of women resides with white women. Hence, in this respect for White women, Africana women activists in America in particular, such as Sojourner Truth ["And Ain't I a Woman"] … Harriet Tubman [Underground Railroad Conductor] … and Ida B. Wells [Anti-Lynching Crusader for Social Justice]…, were pre-feminists, in spite of the fact that the activities of these Africana women did not focus necessarily on women's issues.
>
> (*Africana Womanism 5th & 6th Editions* 13 & 15)

The multidimensionality of Africana Womanism allows the paradigm and theoretical construct to be applied to Africana women, men, and families. The centralization of familyhood indicates a commitment to the collective well-being of Africana people and prioritizes Black women's interdependence with her family and community. In a time when feminist propaganda was excelling and White feminists were opposing family in the White American traditional sense, Hudson (Weems) audaciously reaffirmed Africana women's families as integral to their existence and liberation. "Reclaiming Ourselves" embodies honoring our heritage and protecting our families and legacies.

Throughout her scholarship, Hudson (Weems) demonstrates the utility of an African heritage paradigm that confronts the dynamics of race, class, and gender to support the liberation and upliftment of Africana people. Previous paradigms excluded Black women's issues and struggles or singularly situated Black womanhood in a feminist frame. Such theoretical injustices denied Africana women access to their self and culturally informed pathway to liberation. Rejecting the weak and insufficient terminologies for a philosophy germane to Africana culture proved essential for the Africana womanist struggle for ultimate survival.

Elevating Humanity via Africana Womanism provides a rich overview of the development and foundation of a transformative system, patterned after the victorious humanity of African descended women. Dr. Hudson (Weems)'s journey as a model for Africana womanism creates a homeplace that situates the theory in the lived experiences of Africana people. Her critical analysis over the nearly past four decades has integrated cultural consciousness and social justice as the bedrock for engaging literary and social discourse on the lives of Africana people. To this end, the theoretical construct of Africana Womanism/Africana-Melanated Womanism—grounded in a family-centered framework, wherein race, class, and gender are prioritized—positions Africana people to approach their reality, experiences, and liberation struggle for total justice for all Africana people from a culturally grounded paradigm. Our legacy lives on!

Preface

From Elementary School to High School; Pre-College and University

I.

Tammy Taylor, PhD, Elementary Principal; Co-Founder of *Create & Educate*
Sheka Houston, EdD, Principal & Dir. of Secondary Interventions; Co-founder of *Create & Educate*

> One characteristic of Africana Womanism that we must take our children back to is the concept of Respect. We must begin to not only teach our children that respect is important, but we must also begin to require respect to be given to all, especially our elders. Far greater than any other level of respect, we must teach our youth to have a sense of self-worth and a respect for themselves that motivates them to strive for more in order to attain a level of EXCELLENCE that only comes from putting forth one's very best. Our responsibility is to lead them in the right direction so that they will grow up to become responsible leaders themselves who in turn will pass the lessons on to the future leaders and generations.
>
> (Taylor, *"From Public/Private Schools"* 141)

Africana Womanism is a family-centered ideology that is richly informed by African culture and Afrocentrism. This construct, beautifully fashioned by Dr. Clenora Hudson (Weems), has totally disrupted all previous concepts presented wherein Black women were considered to be feminist, such as Black feminist, African Feminist, Intersectional Feminist, and even Womanist, which Alice Walker herself defines as "…a Black feminist or feminist of color" (xii). Africana Womanism is the first ideology designed for women that does not place gender as the primary concern; the centrality of the family and the community is at the top of the Africana Womanist's list. Hence, the true Africana woman, in virtually all her acts, embodies the Africana Womanist's interconnectedness of their race, class, and gender. This interconnectivity can be traced back to Sojourner Truth's moving speech, "And Ain't I a Woman," where she reiterates the obvious, which is that despite the fact that she is a woman, she receives none of the perks that are lavished upon white women. Therefore, the feminist construct does not fit her circumstance, according to Dr. Hudson (Weems), as her response to the levels of oppression she experiences are based on her unique experiences as a Black woman, who must prioritize the triple plight she suffers. In short, her response is played out through actions of "self-actualization," an observation earlier pointed out in Hudson (Weems)'s first Call for Africana Womanism in the 1989 seminal article in *The Western Journal of Black Studies*, reprinted as Chapter 2 in all subsequent Africana Womanism books. In the final analysis, then, Africana Womanism is a constant reminder of the prioritization Black women must make when faced daily with marginalizations and microaggressions.

In the 1997 iconic literary masterpiece, *Call and Response: The Riverside Anthology of the African American Literary Tradition*, Dr. Hudson (Weems) is referred to as "the first African American woman intellectual to formulate a position on Africana Womanism" (Patricia Liggins Hill, editor, 1811). That position has extolled her as a legendary trend setter, trailblazer, and single authority on the ideology of Africana Womanism. With such expertise, coupled with her decades as mentor to many, both inside and outside the Academy, she has designed this important and useful manuscript as "A Handbook to Elevate Humanity" through the concept of Africana Womanism, which can be experienced through a historical, global, and social justice perspective for women of African descent, as well as her people overall.

For more than three decades, Dr. Hudson (Weems), the progenitor of this international theory, has positively impacted, influenced, and inspired Africana women across generations to be strong women of excellence who represent, in many ways, true family-oriented Warrior Queens. Her relentless and unapologetic quest to empower Black women stems from her dedication and commitment to the Africana community. Her message of hope for the Black family has heralded her as a modern-day heroine, who passionately debunks the idea that Black men are enemies to Black Women, an obvious misinterpretation of the inherent relationship between these intercollective beings. She has made the focus on family a notion that distinguishes the Africana community from other communities highlighting the activities of Black women as having always worked in concert with Black men for true victory for the family. A leader among women across the globe, she has created a concept that, while seemingly simplistic, is very profound in its life-altering nature. For generations to come, Africana Womanism will impact the lives of Black girls and Black women in general, as well as the entire Africana community, as her work will be revered as a legacy for human survival for all.

As co-founders of Create and Educate, LLC, we established for one of our major goals a strong commitment to strengthening the Black family, which is a natural when focusing on students during their early years—elementary, middle, and high school. While a PhD student at the University of South Carolina, Dr. Taylor had the great fortune of meeting Dr. Hudson (Weems) when introduced to the Conceptual Framework of Africana Womanism. Since then, Hudson (Weems) has become a trusted mentor and a friend to our company and our work centering around the family. As educators, we realize the significant role the family plays in developing productive, industrious, and caring children, who are, in essence, genuinely good people. They need only supportive teachers and administrators, working together with their parents in creating the best in them for future possibilities. Therefore, we proudly stand in acknowledgment of the fact that the Africana child is the legacy of the Africana community, as they must continue our rich Africana legacy of collectivity (man, woman, child), a key feature for Africana Womanism. Indeed, with God in front, the salvation for our family is absolute.

II.

The Tale of Two Sisters: Self-Naming Our Struggle and Self-Defining Our Liberation through the Concept of Africana Womanism

Keena Day, EdD, Vice President of Curriculum & Assessment; Consultant, The Savvy Urban Educator, LLC; Treasurer, Colorado Black Women for Political Action

Natalie Lewis, PhD, Vice President of Leadership Development

> The Africana woman, in realizing and properly assessing herself and her movement, properly names herself and her movement. This is a key step, which many women of African descent have unfortunately failed to address for various reasons. Granted, while there are some who have taken the initiative to differentiate their struggle from the White woman's struggle, such as African feminists who differ from the Africana womanist in name only, they have yet to give their struggle its own name.
>
> (Hudson (Weems), *Africana Womanism Fifth Edition* 37)

There has never been a more prudent time in society than now that women identifying as Africana have needed to return to the ancestral and cultural understandings of who we are and the spaces we occupy. While Africana women are increasing their education, owning successful businesses, and moving into senior leadership and C-Suite roles in the workplace, inequities—such as a persistent pay gap, increased maternal death in childbirth, disparities in race, battle fatigue while working in White spaces—continue to plague this progress. As two senior administrators in a school organization, we find that these inequities define our existence as limited leaders, as we experience these kinds of battles daily, although we are oftentimes more educated and represented in scholarship than many of our colleagues. Literally, our sisterhood that has developed has kept us fighting together in pursuit of anti-racist and equitable academic achievements for all students, especially since many of these students represent our memories, triumphs, and struggles as Black people who were once Black students ourselves. As colleagues and as friends, we have agreed in this commitment, and that "Genuine Sisterhood, defined as one of the 18 characteristics of Africana Womanism," is oftentimes what keeps us going, despite the daily struggles with oppression we face.

A perfect example of the challenges in our leadership story took place recently, about a week ago, when a talented Black colleague abruptly quit the job after not feeling seen or heard. This situation led us two, as the top Black women in leadership in our organization, to express the need for our organization to illuminate how Black people sometimes feel. Both of us have different journeys in our experiences as Black people, as Black women, as Black scholars, and as Black leaders, yet we are bonded over the similarities in our treatment as leaders in White-founded and -led organizations. There are countless ways this shows up at work for us: despite not looking similar, as we have been called the others' names; we both have been tone-policed; we both have experienced microaggressions; we both have felt silenced. And so, to help our supervisors and other fellow senior leaders to understand our experiences in order to better understand the need for change, we were asked to share our experiences with this organization of predominantly White leaders. Below is a personal reflection:

> Squeezing my hands together in my lap under the desk, I look back at the mostly white populated room, waiting for my colleague to join me in pouring out our souls. I swallow the rising angst in me having to share my lived narrative about the way that we as a people have been treated (and mostly not seen) during our journey here, particularly as Black women. Trying my hardest in some ways to hide my hurt and vulnerability in that moment, I keep believing that my story is not just my own and that there is a greater purpose than just this moment. (Anonymous)

The story shared is a micro-moment of our experiences as Black women maneuvering a world steeped in whiteness. They just serve as brief examples of realities that Black women face in these contemporary times. Across the US and this world, Black women are forced to struggle, navigating two central components of their identity: being both Black and woman. In this contemporary state, Black women have been receiving degrees at a higher rate in recent years in the US (NCES, 2022) and yet Black women continue to have their voices suppressed and find themselves feeling unseen and passed over for opportunities (Coles & Pasek, 2020). Also significant are their worries about the continued safety of their men and their families (Moniuszko & Bacchus, 2023). In a context that is both post-COVID and ladened with continued oppressive systems and structures, Black women desperately need a framework, centered around the essence of their experiences and identities.

Black women of this modern world are collectively issuing a call, and that needed response is held in the guidance of Africana Womanism.

Not long ago when we were little girls sitting at the knees of our mothers and other elder women, we would listen to their assertions and lessons of how to transition toward womanhood. They would signify solutions with stories about the importance of defining who we were and how we wanted the world to see us. Through the care that they provided us and others, they modeled the centricity of our families and communities at large as our answer, our solution.

With that remembrance of yore in mind, it is time now to reclaim this identity by regrounding ourselves into Africana Womanism and finding our way back to the knowledge of the women before us to assert who we are, what our struggles are, and what our liberation will be. As Dr. Clenora Hudson (Weems) reminds us, we must always separate ourselves from the oppression that plagues our journeys, and reclaim, rename, and redefine these components of our identities for ourselves (Hudson (Weems), *Africana Womanism*, 35). Africana Womanism offers particular characteristics critical to these processes of reclaiming, renaming, and redefining:

1 We are charged with "properly naming ourselves and our movements," which is a critical first step, as Africana Womanists must clearly differentiate ourselves from the movements of others (Hudson (Weems), *Africana Womanism*, 37–38), investing what we must do to engage in a movement specific to our liberation. There is a space for allyship, but we must clearly articulate how our movement is different from that of white normative movements such as feminism. Too often, we neglect this for ourselves by joining the movements of others, but the struggles of Africana Womanists and subsequent liberation from that struggle looks uniquely different for us, as both race and gender contribute to our attempted subjugation.
2 Understanding that in embarking in self-naming both ourselves and our movements, committing to and defining genuine sisterhood in collectively fighting the same battle is also critical. This concept is grounded in Africana Womanism, as the idea of recognizing the reality of our circumstances and how it connects to the woman we call "sister," which helps propel the race forward. In our current time, actual sisterhood in crafting goals and driving toward them together, this is symbolic of how Africana women support each other in all reincarnations of our communities. An example of this is in the sisterhood demonstrated in a common story shared about the mother of the Black Panther icon, Fred Hampton, Iberia, who was an early babysitter for "Bobo," notoriously known as Emmett Till. In fact, Dr. Hudson (Weems) established Till as the true catalyst of the Civil Rights Movement in her 1988 Ford doctoral dissertation, "Emmett Louis Till: The Impetus of the Modern Civil Rights Movement," (U of Iowa), later published as *Emmett Till: The Sacrificial Lamb of the Civil Rights Movement*,

1994. Hampton recalled how his mother reacted to Mamie Till losing her son and how that impacted his understanding of racism as a child (Haas 17). This demonstration of how we care for one another as sisters is characteristic of Africana women.

3 Making family the central driver of our movements as Africana Womanists is critical. We are in concert with the Black male, who is not our enemy. While feminism as a theory positions itself as a movement against patriarchy as a barrier to power, Africana womanism does not pit itself against our men. Rather, as Africana Womanists, we align ourselves with Black men within the liberation struggle as the heart of Africana womanism. This ideology in and of itself centers within the African world view of "both/and" instead of "either/or." In other words, we see ourselves as a collective, not as individuals (Hudson (Weems), *Africana Womanism*).

These are just a few of the 18 features of Africana Womanism, but they provide a strong start for engaging in our movement. For Africana Womanists to firmly perform the charge that Sojourner Truth emphatically impressed upon women to come together and "turn the world back right side up again," it is imperative that we reclaim, rename, and redefine what liberation will look like because of engaging in these essential characteristics. This handbook will serve as a starting point for reengaging for some and introducing to others the hallmarks of Africana Womanism features. This book serves as the blueprint for our work to come forth to march our people toward true liberation.

Introduction

It is critical to first note that Africana Womanism is evolving, terminologically only, to include a new name, BRONZE WOMANISM, and holds to the principle that the names here (Africana Womanism; Africana-Melanated Womanism; Africana-Melanated/Bronze Womanism) neither connote nor denote a conceptual difference. The Fifth and Sixth Edition of *Africana Womanism: Reclaiming Ourselves* introduce five new chapters in Part III: "From Africana Womanism to Africana-Melanated Womanism,"

> This new section offers new materials for new insights into the natural evolution of Africana Womanism to Africana-Melanated womanism, convincingly presenting a rationale that explicates the basic commonalities existing between all melanated women. Initially creating Africana Womanism as a realistic paradigm for all women of African descent …, addressing the underline message within the context of our own cultural, historic and current matrix, I now move to a broader more overt collective, including other women of a more diverse backgrounds whose identity is also rooted in blackness. Hence, since the inception of Africana Womanism in the mid 1980s, it now hails as a more overt inclusive terminology reflecting its more inclusive concept. In short, it has become the embodiment of inherent conceptual and terminological inclusivity. Aubrey Bruce [contends that new term was]—"birthed from Africana Womanism."
>
> *(Africana Womanism 5th and 6th Editions* 93 & 107)

With that said, we can now move forward, understanding fully that no lengthy explication for the definition of Africana Womanism versus Africana-Melanated womanism, now evolving to Bronze Womanism, is required, as the terms are used interchangeably. Indeed, relative to the commonality relative to all three terms, ethnicity and color remain the very foundation of the concept. It's just that the nuances and the history of a term sometimes call for periodic reconsideration, since one strives toward selecting the most complete and comprehensive terminology, particularly when refining the dynamics of a movement. Be that as it may, in the final analysis, the main question is

DOI: 10.4324/9781032720036-1

what are the benefits to be gained by the Africana Womanist, the Africana-Melanated Womanist, or the Bronze Womanist, including her family? Further, by extension, what can the concept itself offer society in general? In the Foreword to *Africana-Melanated Womanism: In It Together*, Rev. Dr. Debora Jackson, the Stoddard Professor of Management and Dean of the Business School at Worcester Polytechnic Institute, MA, contemplates a possible resolution for today's urgent human problem, and its relativity to this growing global paradigm:

> Is there a way out of the morass that has left us fractured, distressed and despairing? I believe that there is, and this way is found in the theory and praxis of Africana Womanism. Our times demand a way forward that is both healing and restorative. A focus is required that helps societies function inclusively and holistically to ensure that all are served, and none are left behind. As scholar, author, and leader, Dr. Clenora Hudson (Weems), brilliantly demonstrates, Africana-Melanated Womanism speaks to our most urgent needs as a society, and this work provides a necessary and instructive hope for such a time as this.
>
> (Jackson, Foreword to *Africana-Melanated Womanism* x–xi)

As Africana Womanism marked the first publication, and the longest-lived terminology for the theory itself, for simplicity, I will stick with that terminology. The very *raison d'être* for this book, ***Elevating Humanity via Africana Womanism***—a brief, though comprehensive manuscript, designed to deliver a critical message, relative to what Africana Womanism is, as well as identifying the role of the Africana Womanist—centers around the mission and commitment of both to Africana people in general. Africana Womanism is an authentic family-centered paradigm, not the traditional female-centered construct characterizing feminism. It prioritizes the tripartite plight of Africana women—racism, classism, and sexism—unlike Black feminism, that speaks of the simultaneity of these obstacles for Black women. Neither is it Womanism, which Alice Walker herself defines as "a Black feminist or feminist of color," nor is it African feminism, which differs only in terminology. Thus, without any competition to existing female-based theoretical books, this book, unique and separate from all other female-based concepts, could serve as an excellent companion to the definitive Africana Womanism book, as well as the other Africana Womanism books, which can serve as a brief guide for transforming humanity to a higher level, one that promotes social justice for all humankind. To validate its potential, the foundational source for this book is the original 1993 classic text *Africana Womanism: Reclaiming Ourselves*, reprinted by Routledge in 2019/2020, with a new section, Part III, "From Africana Womanism to Africana-Melanated Womanism." Giving credence to this new fresh companion book is the fact that its originality and, moreover, its conceptualizer were announced by the editors of a major national anthology,

Call and Response: The Riverside Anthology of the African American Literary Tradition (1997), who contended that

> The first African American woman intellectual to formulate a position on Africana Womanism was Clenora Hudson (Weems), author of the 1993 groundbreaking study, *Africana Womanism: Reclaiming Ourselves.* Taking a strong position that black women should not pattern their liberation after Eurocentric feminism but after the historic and triumphant women of African descent, Hudson (Weems) has launched a new critical discourse in the Black Women's Literary Movement.
>
> (Liggins Hill, *Call and Response: The Riverside Anthology of the African American Literary Tradition*, 1811)

This first short Africana Womanism book, with its distinct purpose—"To Elevate Humanity"—poses no real competition to any of the other Africana/Africana-Melanated Womanism books. Rather, this text is an added feature, which can, in fact, initiate a package of two distributions, together enhancing the readership of Africana Womanism texts by introducing new readers to the topic, while satisfying its already established readers. The overviews presented by the writers for the preliminary materials—Foreword, Preface, Epilogue, and Afterword—give an excellent summation of the very essence, the *raison d'être*, of the true Africana womanist.

Elevating Humanity via Africana Womanism—brevity aimed at reaching a broader community, both inside and outside Academe—is steeped in deep thought, designed to lay out, in a nutshell, the rich life and legacy of the Africana womanist, particularly focusing on her responsibility in upholding our commitment to the family, with the foreknowledge that our destiny as an Africana people is interconnected. The theory of Africana Womanism, which is family-centered, embraces the entire family (men, women, and children), a rich legacy dating back to African antiquity. Amid today's uncertainties, there is the urgent need to re-call our traditional practice of Collectivity in the struggle against racial dominance. Our ultimate survival as human beings must be our top priority, indeed, a necessity for bringing to full fruition ultimate salvation for all humankind. Critical to enabling Africana women to do our part, we must first understand that we have a responsibility to ourselves and to all humankind, and that in order to respect our true roles, we must first recognize our true nature, which is undergirded in the 18 characteristics of Africana/Africana Womanism:

> Self-Namer; Self Definer; Family Centered; Strong (physical, spiritual & emotional strength); Genuine in Sisterhood; In Concert with the Man in the Liberation Struggle; Spiritual; Whole; Authentic; Respected; Recognized; Flexible Role Players; Male Compatible; Respectful of Elders; Adaptable; Ambitious; Mothering and Nurturing

Definitions for each of these elements are presented in Part I of the seminal Chapters 3 and 4, wherein a rhyming couplet follows the naming of each of the 18 Africana Womanism features.

Elevating Humanity via Africana Womanism focuses on the Africana woman, which is more of a terminological evolution, though also a contextual evolution to some degree, as it connotes a broad ethnic inclusivity more overtly. To be sure, the Africana womanist continues to operate within the context of her own unique daily activities in a world that subjugates not only her, but her entire family as well. Although endless efforts on the part of the dominant culture to relegate her to a lower level of existence and respectability, she remains resolute in her rejection of the racist mindset, insisting on reclaiming our birthright to first properly name and define ourselves as the first step in refining a paradigm relative to our unique lives. A clarion call for this movement was issued forth in the mid-eighties, assigning the name Africana Womanism, along with its 18 descriptors. Herein lies the multi-roles of the Africana womanist to actualize the idea and to bring to full fruition truth, justice, and victory to her family, and by extension the global Africana community.

This manuscript consists of two parts and a Final Coda: **Part I**—"Africana Womanism: The Flipside of the Human Coin"—has four (4) chapters. Chapter 1—"Africana Womanism: What It Is/What It Ain't"—offers a clear definition of the concept. Chapter 2—"Cultural and Agenda Conflicts in Academia: Critical Issues for Women's Studies"—is the Clarion Call for Africana Womanism to come forth and act. Chapters 3 and 4 list and expound on the 18 characteristics of the Africana Womanist and her male counterpart, respectively. **Part II**, "Social Justice Overdue: Standing Strong—In It Together"—also contains four chapters, beginning with Chapter 5—"Debunking Excuses for Racism: Africana Legendaries from A to Z"—which introduces 26 legendary Africana people from A to Z: 21 are women, because of the book's focus and the remaining 5 are Africana men, representing our natural interconnectivity. Chapter 6 highlights poetry, short and powerful. The first section opens with commentary on the memorable foul name-calling, "Nappy-Headed Hos," of the Black basketball women athletes at Rutgers University by a national syndicated television and radio talk show host, Don Imus, in April 2007. Responding to this offensive incident, I wrote several poems, commenting on Racism and Misogyny against the Black Family, which is the title of the chapter, followed by three new poems, issuing forth what must be the mindset for our family in general. The second part of the poetry chapter, "From the Bible to Streets", presents the Africana Womanism Trilogy, commenting on the importance of collectivity for Africana men and women in their fight against racism. Chapter 7—"James Baldwin and Toni Morrison: Literary Crusaders for Social Justice"—presents these two as international iconic literary *activists*, both artists and activists, who have left us an invaluable literary legacy aimed at bringing to fruition true social justice for Africana people.

Then comes Chapter 8, the **Conclusion**, offering an informative overview, which includes an objective assessment of the theory of Africana Woman, by a white male colleague: "Until you have the right to give a name to yourself and to what you are doing, you have no power whatsoever. Africana womanism is a fine idea." The end of the Conclusion offers a Self-Evaluation, wherein there is invaluable commentary, pin-pointing Thoughts, Suggestions, and Considerations. This brief section is followed by the **Final Coda**, representing the voice of the new millennium, which is presented by two of my graduating seniors, who situate commonly considered circumstances in particular areas of research/study. The first one comes from the field of Social Work, and the second one focuses on the Responsibility of Society to the Children, and in this case, Black girls. That said, it is very important to acknowledge the seminal role of the endorsers, whose insightful commentaries facilitate in protecting and enhancing the vast potential of the readership of this brief, though very important 100-page-manuscript, including the preliminary material.

Part I

Africana Womanism

"The Flipside" of the Human "Coin"

Africana Womanism [a family centered concept] … establishes an authentic race-based Africana theory of prioritizing race, class, and gender for all women of African descent … Black men and women must move forward together, or the race will self-destruct.

(Aldridge in Hudson-Weems' The Definitive Emmett Till 151–152)

"Africana Womanism: I Got Your Back, Boo"

Don't you know by now, girl, we're all In It Together!
Family-Centrality--that's it; we're going nowhere without the other,
That means the men, the women, and children, too,
Truly collectively working—**"I got your back, Boo."….**

(Clenora Hudson --1st of 4 stanzas of Hudson-Weems' 2009 poem)

DOI: 10.4324/9781032720036-2

1 Africana Womanism

What It Is/What It Ain't

> Neither an outgrowth nor an addendum to feminism, *Africana Womanism* is not Black feminism, African feminism, or Walker's womanism that some Africana women have come to embrace. *Africana Womanism* is an ideology created and designed for all women of African descent. It is grounded in African culture, and therefore, it necessarily focuses on the unique experiences, struggles, needs, and desires of Africana women. It critically addresses the dynamics of the conflict between the mainstream feminist, the Black feminist, the African feminist, and the Africana womanist. The conclusion is that *Africana Womanism* and its agenda are unique and separate from both White feminism and Black feminism, and moreover, to the extent of naming in particular, *Africana Womanism* differs from African feminism.
>
> (Hudson (Weems), *Africana Womanism 5th & 6th Editions*)

With the above clarification of what *Africana Womanism is*—which evolved terminologically to Africana Womanism—and what it *is not*, the urgent question, then, is simply this: Why is Africana Womanism/Africana-Melanated Womanism/Bronze Womanism critical to the ultimate survival of humanity? The first thing that comes to mind is that in order to properly address one's own needs, it is important to first distinguish oneself from others, and in this case, others' names, and theoretical concepts. In other words, it's about our own goals and our own collective objectives. I am here reminded of an earlier publication, delivered at the First International Conference on Women of Africa and the African Diaspora, held at the University of Nigeria-Nsukka in 1992, and published six years later in *Sisterhood, Feminisms and Power: From Africa to the Diaspora* (1997). According to Dr. Daphne Ntiri in the Introduction to *Africana Womanism: Reclaiming Ourselves*,

> Hudson (Weems)' presentation received serious attention from panelists and participants alike at the Nigeria meeting. Her diligent portrayal of the historical facts that have systematically marginalized women of African descent—even the African woman in her own land—drove home some hard facts and opened the eyes of the women to new intellectual realms.

DOI: 10.4324/9781032720036-3

> As Chair of the Panel on Women and Ideologies where Hudson (Weems) presented, I noted large-scale concurrence from Africana womanists in the standing-room-only crowd. The heartening response to Africana Womanism was a strong indicator of acceptance, timeliness and appropriateness of theme. The audience, which included women from the United States, Canada, Nigeria, South Africa, Jamaica, Brazil, England and many other countries, were loud in their applause and support of *Africana Womanism*. Endless interviews and newspaper stories marked the symbolic importance of the new movement. *The Nigeria Daily Times,* with its headlines, "Africana Womanism: Beyond Bra Burning," of Monday, July 27, 1992, contributed to globalizing the concept and endorsing this new action:
>
> Personal and racial experiences … will be the factors responsible for the evolution of Africana Womanism. Therefore, legitimate concerns of the Africana Woman are issues to be addressed within the context of African culture and history. Africana Womanists do not believe in "bra burning." They believe in womanhood, the family and society. (*Daily Times*, 1992)
>
> This landmark pioneering treatise of Africana woman's realities cannot be ignored. With seeds planted on fertile soil, the harvest will be bountiful. It will unlock closed doors and usher in a spirit of renewed plentitude.
>
> (Ntiri, Introduction in *Africana Womanism 5th & 6th Editions*, 7–8 & 8–9)

As the presentation/article reveal, there are many of us, Africana people, who find the priorities of the dominant culture problematic, since they conflict with our priorities, such as family centrality, indeed, a major cornerstone for our lives:

> Both men and women—… in their efforts to remain authentic in their existence, such as prioritizing their needs, even if the needs are not of primary concern for the dominant culture … [question,] in the midst of oppression, human suffering and death—the empowerment of women and individualism over human dignity and rights. … Granted, the prioritizing of female empowerment and gender issues may be justifiable for those women who have not been plagued by powerlessness based on ethnic differences; however, that is certainly not the case for those who are Africana women.
>
> (Hudson (Weems), *"Africana Womanism" in Sisterhood* 149–150)

This difference in priorities compelled me to consider the history of Africana people, relative to women in particular, as the focus on female empowerment, instead of race empowerment, is not the first priority in our communities. Hence, the proper name to be assigned to us, reflecting our reality, cannot be the same as that of the dominant culture, which was already cast, designed for and by white women.

Africana Womanism, an entirely different name, and agenda for us, takes me back to its very beginnings, even before the terminology itself. African Womanism evolved from the recognition of a long-standing authentic practice on the part of women of African descent, dating back to African antiquity, who needed only to be properly named and officially defined, as dictated by our own unique historical and cultural matrix. In other words, we need a paradigm that accurately reflects our true life experiences, needs, and desires, including the co-existence of Africana men and women, who experience shared oppression, and, thus, who must operate in a collective struggle for the survival of our families and communities. "It's a family affair," and has always been, wherein we "stick together," indeed, "for better or for worse." Sounds familiar? Indeed, for we have always been family centered, not female or otherwise centered. Hence, below is the process by which this phenomenon took shape, wherein I refined it after naming and defining it by openly acknowledging its pre-existence in yet another article in *Sisterhood*:

> For nearly a decade, I have been actively working on naming and defining, via identifying and refining an African-centered paradigm for women of African descent. In observing the traditional role, character, and activity of this collective group, identified by their common African ancestry, I concluded during the early stages of my research that the phenomenon I named and defined as Africana Womanism had long been in existence, dating back to the rich legacy of African womanhood. Therefore, I did not create the phenomenon in and of itself, but rather observed Africana women, documented our reality, and refined a paradigm relative to who we are, what we do, and what we believe in as a people.
>
> (Hudson (Weems), *"Self-Naming"* 449)

The activities surrounding Africana Womanism itself commenced in the fall of 1985, my first semester as a Ford doctoral student at the University of Iowa, during which time I challenged feminism for Black women, which was designed for and by white women to address their particular demands, and, by extension, Black feminism, which suggested its affinity with the concept of feminism. I initially called my theory "Black Womanism," which later evolved to Africana Womanism, as I wanted to include Africa in its name. For the next three years, from 1985 to 1988, with my culminating first publication on the subject in late 1989, I relentlessly spoke out on this crucial subject at national conferences. However, that litany of presentations for me began in the fall of 1985 with an Iowa City local television program, *The Silver Tongue*, where I debated with a whole panel of feminists, Black and White. It was engaging and I left feeling quite satisfied, knowing, from the responses, that Black/Africana Womanism was well received. That following semester, I spoke at the March 13–16, 1986, National Council for Black Studies (NCBS) Annual Conference in Boston, where I spearheaded the panel, which I set up—"Black Feminism—Racism First, Sexism Last: The Survival of the Black Race." I insisted that early Black women activists, like Sojourner Truth, Harriet Tubman, and Ida B. Wells were not pre-feminists, but rather pre-Africana Womanists. The following year, I spoke again on Africana Womanism at the April 7–9, 1987, NCBS Conference, in Philadelphia and later at the April 28–30, 1987, African Heritage Studies Association Annual Conference. Both were wonderfully received! In fact, some of my colleagues admitted that feminism, for some reason or another, did not quite work for them, and they expressed their gratitude for this new direction/distinction. In June 1987, I set up a panel under the title "The Tripartite Plight of Black Women," for the National Women's Studies Association Convention, which was held in Atlanta, Georgia, on the Spelman College campus. During that fall semester, I continued to challenge Black feminism in a paper I presented at a 1987 University of Iowa Black Survival Conference, which I titled "Black Womanism versus Black Feminism: A Critical Issue for Human Survival." Following those national conferences, I accepted an invitation to set up another panel on the theory for the National Women's Studies Association Conference, held at the University of Minnesota that following summer, 1988.

The fruition of this long continuous work culminated in two publications. The first and most important one, "Cultural and Agenda Conflicts in Academia: Critical Issues for Africana Women's Studies," was released in the 1989 winter issue of *The Western Journal of Black Studies*. This was the urgent call for a new terminology for articulating the historical and cultural reality of women of African descent:

> Africana women might begin by naming and defining their unique movement "Africana Womanism." The concept of Womanism can be traced back to Sojourner's [1852] speech that began to develop and highlight Africana women's unique experience into a paradigm for Africana women. *Africana Womanism* does not suggest that female subjugation is the most critical issue they face in their struggle for parity. Like Black feminism, *Africana Womanism* acknowledges societal gender problems as critical issues to be resolved; however, it views feminism, the suggested alternative to these problems, as a sort of inverted White patriarchy, with the White feminist now in command and on top. Mainstream feminism is women's co-opting themselves into mainstream patriarchal values.
>
> (Hudson (Weems), *"Cultural and Agenda Conflicts"* 187)

Also in December 1989, that second article, "The Tripartite Plight of African American Women as Reflected in the Novels of Zora Neale Hurston and Alice Walker," was released in the *Journal of Black Studies*. This new terminology, coupled with a completely new paradigm, expressed a distinct discontent with other female-based constructs, such as feminism, black feminism, and womanism, which had not proposed a true and appropriate agenda for Africana women, relative to the prioritization of our triple plight—Race, Class, and Gender.

In 1993, approximately four years later, *Africana Womanism: Reclaiming Ourselves* was released by Bedford Publishers, wherein one of the seminal chapters, "The Agenda of the Africana Womanist" (revised), lays out the basis of the authentic Africana Womanism paradigm. Africana Womanism, indeed, controversial, was the new kid on the block. It was a brand-new concept, documenting the historical and ongoing reality of who Black women really are and how we address daily racial issues impacting our multi-dimensional lives. In the Foreword to *Africana Womanism: Reclaiming Ourselves*, the late Dr. 'Zula Sofola, renowned international scholar, and Nigeria's first female playwright, made the following assessment:

> *Africana Womanism: Reclaiming Ourselves* is not simply a scholarly work, one of those in the mainstream, but our own. It is a new trail blazed with incontrovertible revelations on the African heritage and gender question. Hudson (Weems) bravely takes the bull by the horns, confronts the Eurocentric avalanche of works on questions of gender, and puts forward the Afrocentric point of view.
>
> (Sofola, *Foreword in Africana Womanism 5th & 6th Editions*, xi)

Around the same time, noted black psychologist, Dr. Julia Hare—spouse of Dr. Nathan Hare, who launched the nation's first Department of Black Studies at San Francisco State University in the late sixties—made a profound commentary on the reality of the difference in the politics of Black life and that of white life, particularly in terms of the difference in issues relative to women in the two groups:

> Women who are calling themselves black feminists need another word that describes what their concerns are. Black feminism in not a word that describes the plight of black women. In fact, … black feminists have not even come together and come to a true core definition of what black feminism is. The white race has a woman problem because the women were oppressed [suppressed]. Black people have a man and woman problem because Black men are as oppressed as their women.
>
> (Hare, *Quoted in Black Issues* 15)

Hare's 1993 call for another name for the black woman's movement, because of the problematic dynamics of the prevalent existing terminologies, such as the various forms of feminisms, suggests that there is a definite need for a new terminology and concept, hence the significance of self-naming, and, by extension, self-definition for the integrity and survival of Africana people. While her call indicates that she was unaware of the existence of the concept of Africana Womanism, which she soon came to know, her statement was both powerful and true, strongly echoing the underlying theory of Africana Womanism in the ongoing debate, both within and beyond the Academy. But what is particularly disturbing, on the other hand, is the dominant culture's failure to acknowledge certain proper names, identifications, and systems, such as Africana Womanism. Instead, the dominant culture usually promotes Western theoretical concepts that mirror theirs. In other words, it promotes mainstream constructs, signaled using an identification with Western terminology, such as feminism, as the model for all others. Those others, then, must follow the mandates, thereby creating a duplicate, rather than initiating their own authentic paradigm to stop the one constancy in an ever-changing climate of dissension and confusion revolving around the very lives and destinies of an oppressed people. In commanding a different terminology to reflect a different culture, this proper self-naming and self-defining will at the same time offer the first step toward correcting confusion and misconception regarding one's identity and the true level of one's struggle in terms of an authentic agenda. Hare's statement, then, reflects the nuances of the relativity of a particular terminology and concept, feminism, issued forth by white women, whose agenda and priorities are not necessarily suited for all. Obviously, feminism does not work for Black women; nor does it work for our male counterparts, given the fact that we are both trapped first and foremost based on our race, thus the race factor, rather than the gender factor, so prevalently addressed today. To be sure, the survival of the whole, that being the people, is bigger and more important than placing gender as the top priority. In fact, some white women, too, are beginning to agree that the gender issue, and in this case the woman, is not more important than the whole—humanity. Hence, there is this crucial need for self-naming and self-defining, with our own set of priorities, for in giving name to a particular thing, it simultaneously gives it true meaning, indeed, the first step in speaking our truth into existence.

That said, in 1997, the editors of *Call and Response: The Riverside Anthology of the African American Literary Tradition*, which is a major anthology for Black literature, made their assessment of Africana Womanism in the biographical headnote to my contribution to that anthology:

> The first African American woman intellectual to formulate a position on Africana Womanism was Clenora Hudson (Weems), author of the 1993 groundbreaking study, *Africana Womanism: Reclaiming Ourselves*. Taking a strong position that black women should not pattern their liberation after Eurocentric feminism but after the historic and triumphant women of African descent, Hudson (Weems) has launched a new critical discourse in the Black Women's Literary Movement.
>
> (Liggins Hill 1811)

In my article, "Africana Womanism: An Historical, Global Perspective for Women of African Descent," I opened with Sojourner Truth's famous oration, "And Ain't I a Woman," expressed at a white Woman's Convention in Akron, Ohio, in which the prioritization of race, class, and gender takes center stage. Her self-actualization speech exemplifies her position, for she was forced to first address the race factor, and then the class factor, before she could even begin to entertain the notion of female subjugation, the gender factor:

> Well, children, where there is so much racket there must be something out of kilter. I think that 'twixt the Negroes of the South and the women at the North, all talking about rights, the white men will be in a fix pretty soon. But what's all this here talking about? That man over there says that women need to be helped into carriages, and lifted over ditches, and to have the best place everywhere. Nobody ever helps me into carriages, or over mud puddles, or gives me any best place! And ain't I a woman?
>
> (Sojourner Truth 1851)

That was at an 1852 National White Women's Conference in Akron, Ohio, where Sojourner was not welcomed because of her color. Instead, she was shunned by the Community of Women with whom she fallaciously thought she had an affinity. Even today, traces of such sentiments reign, though not as pronounced as then.

National and international publications and presentations continued. In 2004, *Africana Womanist Literary Theory*, the sequel to *Africana Womanism: Reclaiming Ourselves*, was published by Africa World Press. Moreover, the 1993 classic was later published in 2020 by Routledge Press as the Fifth Edition, introducing a new section, Part III, "From Africana Womanism to Africana Womanism." This section consists of five new chapters, including Chapter 11, "Africana Womanism's Race, Class and Gender: Pre-Intersectionality." It was a reminder of the fact that the concept, with its distinct meanings and specified terminology—such as "connectedness/connectivity," relative to the prioritizing of the triple plight of Africana women (race, class, and gender)—is a major cornerstone of Africana Womanism, which was launched even before "Intersectionality," later advancing to the concept of "Intersectional Feminism." According to Dr. Mark Christian in the Afterword to *Africana Womanism: Reclaiming Ourselves,* Fifth Edition,

> The current academic fad phrase is "intersectionality" as if those of us in Africana discourse never considered the myriad of issues encountered by our communities. "Race," class and gender, and the prioritization therein, have always been key issues for comprehending Africana Womanism.
>
> (Christian 131 & 151)

Indeed, specific terms had been appended to Africana Womanism to connect the nature of the basic areas of oppression with the Black woman, thereby demonstrating how collectivity and connectivity relate directly to both the subjects (the individuals) and the foundational basis undergirding the oppressive forces obtruded upon Africana people. In the final analysis, the theory of Africana Womanism proved early on to be more appropriate for analyzing the reality of Africana women, and by extension Africana life. As the salient debate on Africana Womanism versus Intersectionality is boldly addressed in this chapter, wherein both its origins and its impact on Africana women are brought to the forefront, the rhetorical question, then, is "Are there benefits of intersectionality for Black women?"

> Today, the current emphasis on the relativity of feminist activity, called "intersectionality," which was introduced by race theorist, Kimberlie Crenshaw in 1989, has enhanced the dominance of the application of the Eurocentric tool of analysis [feminism] for Black life. Clearly this is not necessary, as an Afrocentric tool of analysis for Black life, particularly relative to Black women and their families, was already in place with the earlier advent of Africana Womanism.
>
> (Hudson (Weems), *"Africana Womanism's race, class and gender: Pre-Intersectionality"* 107 & 123)

Obviously, the term intersectionality is limiting for Black women, since both "feminism" and, by extension, "Intersectional Feminism" emerged from outside the domain of the Black population, having been initiated and hence defined by white women. In fact, of all the possible motives behind this concept for Black women, as suggested in the quotations above and below, only the last one could have a positive component, which is to serve as a corrective for historical wrongs, particularly for Black women, historically excluded from and unwelcomed by white women:

> In making feminism more inclusive, while appealing to a larger audience, intersectionality was strategically introduced. Traditional feminism since its inception, until the terminology intersectionality was introduced in 1989, was gender exclusive, which now advocates an interest in racism and classism, too ... On the other hand, feminism and its current evolution from gender exclusivity to intersectionality was designed for and by White women, ... its motive is perhaps as a means of swelling the numbers of supporters by expanding its agenda, or by addressing, on some level, its unjust practice of racial dominance.
>
> (Hudson (Weems), *"Africana Womanism's race, class and gender: Pre-Intersectionality"* 108–109 & 24–25)

Most recently, the publication of the first US-based edited volume on Africana Womanism, *Africana-Melanated Womanism: In It Together*, was released in 2022. The following is a succinct summary of the end result, relative to the question of Africana Womanism versus Intersectionality.

> Yes, intersectionality, a step in the right direction, expanding beyond gender issues alone, is quite appropriate in defining white women in their 3rd and even 4th Waves of Feminism today, evolving from gender [female]-exclusivity to current inclusivity. However, it clearly offers nothing new or particularly positive for Africana women and their communities.
>
> (Hudson (Weems), *Africana-Melanated Womanism* 20)

As history cannot be dismissed, one must wonder, then, if remnants of the past are still lurking. Toni Morrison, Nobel laureate, updates us in her 1971 *New York Times Magazine* article, "What the Black Woman Thinks about Women's Lib," challenging the participants and the leaders of the Women's Lib Movement of the searing sixties:

> The Early Image of Women's Lib was of an elitist organization made up of upper-middle class [white] women with the concerns of that class and not paying much attention to the problems of most black women. Too much emphasis is placed on gender politics.
>
> (Morrison 63)

Of course, this was ten years before Betty Friedan, author of *The Feminine Mystique* (1961)—which was the definitive book, establishing the position of white women in the throes of the Women's Lib Movement—reassessed her position of female exclusivity 20 years later in *The Second Stage* (1981). Indeed, this change was very positive for Friedan, changing her initial position of female centrality to family centrality. She also called for ending "male-bashing," which was characteristic of feminism prior to this, as white women openly stated that their number one enemy is the white male. Morrison, of course, expounded on that issue in her same article, affirming that

> For years black women accepted that rage, even regarded that acceptance as their unpleasant duty. But in so doing they frequently kicked back, and they seem never to have become the true slaves that White women see in their own history.
>
> (Morrison 63)

The following year, Black sociologist Joyce Ladner, author of *Tomorrow's Tomorrow*, takes it a bit further, contending that "Black women do not perceive their enemy to be black men, but rather the enemy is considered to be oppressive forces in the larger society which subjugate black men, women and children" (277–278). Ladner later endorsed *Africana Womanism: Reclaiming Ourselves*:

> Hudson (Weems) examines the perceptions women in the African diaspora have of their historical and contemporary roles. It is within this comparative framework that the work advances the state of knowledge on the lives of women of color.
>
> (Ladner, *Book Endorsement* 1993)

Then there was the opinion of the Black man, many of whom agree with the idea of the importance of Black men and women working together, thereby invalidating those who don't. According to Black sociologist Clyde Franklin II, "Black men are relatively powerless in this country, and their attempts at domination, aggression, and the like, while sacrificing humanity, are ludicrous" (112). Today, Africana women must understand and insist that, as their reality has demonstrated, they are equal partners in a relationship in which passive female subjugation neither *was* nor *is* the norm in our community. I referenced South Africa in the first chapter of *Africana-Melanated Womanism*, titled "The Significance of an Authentic Africana Womanism Paradigm: Collectivity and Interconnectedness for Social Justice," in which

> ...we witnessed a perceptive article by a South African journalist, Gracious Madondo, in *The Southern Times: The Newspaper for Southern Africa*, wherein she expounds on the question as to "Why Africa Relates to Africana Womanism?" Here she highlights the male-female co-existence, dating back to pre-colonialism in Africa: "Unlike the Western rooted feminist approach ... Africana womanism speaks of male and female compatibility where men and women co-exist together without conflict" (Madondo, 2018) ... Dr. Hudson (Weems)' analysis, too, goes back to African antiquity.
>
> (Madondo in Hudson (Weems)' *Africana-Melanated Womanism* 5)

While Madondo makes an excellent case as to "why Africa relates to Africana Womanism," given its roots dating back to before the advent of the invasion of colonialism in Africa, one must remember that this paradigm was created for Africana women by an Africana woman. It was designed to address our varied needs, which are not necessarily those of women of other ethnicities. My position, then, is that

> While I am not calling for a replacement of traditional, established paradigms, such as feminism, etc., for they were, indeed, created out of the needs of a particular group that had legitimate concerns or issues that needed to be addressed, I am nonetheless proposing for a broadening of the

> body of criticism to include *yet* another perspective and paradigms, which is Africana Womanism, now evolving to Africana-Melanated Womanism.
>
> (*Africana Womanism* 112 & 129)

Hence, I ask the following rhetoric question: Is it not plausible for women of African descent to likewise address their legitimate needs, as well as those of her family, which includes the men and the children as well? The question is obviously rhetorical, as this is exactly what the theory of Africana Womanism does and, moreover, must continue to do for the ultimate survival the entire global Africana family?

> On that note on the relativity of inherent Connectivity and Collectivity characterizing Africana Womanism and the dynamics of the two-sided Human Coin (the man and the woman), our position must remain family centered, as clarified by Dr. Sofola in her 1992 international conference presentation, "Feminism and the Psyche of African Womanhood." Distinguishing Africana women from feminism, she holds that
>
> The world view of the African is rooted in the philosophy of holistic harmony and communalism, rather than in the individualistic isolationism of Europe. The principle of relatedness is the *sine qua non* of African social reality.
>
> (Sofola, *quoted in Africana Womanism*, 39 & 41)

Granted, Africana Womanism acknowledges that we do have traditional roles, although flexible, as observed in the theory of Africana Womanism, but neither role is inferior to the other. With that in mind, I propose, then, that we remain resolute in defining Who We Are and Who We Will Not Be! As we continue our "strive toward freedom," as Dr. Martin Luther King, Jr., asserts, for ultimate Social Justice, I pledge to continue my duties as a participant—"Speaking Truth to Power"—in my ongoing publications and speaking engagements on Africana Womanism, the flip side of the human coin. For example, during the four-year-plus pandemic hiatus, I published the following books:

> *Africana Womanism: Reclaiming Ourselves, Fifth Edition (2020)*
>
> *Africana Paradigms, Practices/Literary Texts: Evoking Social Justice (2021)*
>
> *Africana-Melanated Womanism: In It Together (2022)*
>
> *Africana Womanism: Reclaiming Ourselves, Sixth Edition (2023)*

Moreover, as the progenitor of Africana Womanism, I delivered the Opening Keynote Address, *Why Africana Womanism? Authenticity and Collectivity for Social Justice*, for the University of Zimbabwe's 2021 Women's Conference, an outgrowth of its 2010 First International Africana Womanism Conference.

Finally, as the Ida Beam Distinguished Visiting Professor (2021–2022), I delivered the Keynote Address *Africana Womanism: Nobel Laureate Toni Morrison as a Model Africana Womanist Artivist for Social Justice* for the 50th Anniversary of African American Studies at my alma mater, the University of Iowa, where I was a National Ford Pre-Doctoral Fellow, whose doctoral dissertation, "Emmett Louis Till: The Impetus of the Modern Civil Rights Movement" (1988), later published as *Emmett Till: The Sacrificial Lamb of the Civil Rights Movement* (1994), established Till, the flip side of the human coin, as the true catalyst of the Civil Rights Movement.

With that in mind, let us be ever mindful that it takes "two to tango," and that our goal as an Africana people is to ensure that our legacy is passed on to our children, and to our future generations. Below is the 2009 poem, dedicated to all Africana people:

Don't you know by now, girl, we're all In It Together!
Family-Centrality—that's it; we're going nowhere /out the other.
That means the men, the women, and children, too,
Truly collectively working—"I got your back, Boo."

Racism means the violation of our constitutional rights,
Which creates on-going legal, and even physical fights;
This 1st priority for humankind is doing what it must do,
Echoing our 1st lady, Michelle—"I got your back, Boo."

Classism is the hoarding of financial privileges,
Privileges we must all have now in pursuit of happiness.
Without a piece of financial pie, we're doomed to have a coup;
Remember—protect the other—"I got your back, Boo."

Sexism, the final abominable sin of female subjugation,
A battle we must wage right now to restore our family relations.
All forms of sin inevitably fall under 1 of the 3 offenses:
A.M.W., "I Got Your Back, Boo," corrects our common senses.

(Hudson, *"Africana Womanism: I Got Your Back, Boo"* FEB 2009)

"To God Be the Glory."

2 "Cultural & Agenda Conflicts in Academia

Critical Issues for Africana Women's Studies"[1]

> Well, chillun, whar dar is so much racket, dar must be something out o' kilter. I t'ink dat 'twixt de niggers of de Souf an' de women at de Norf all a-talkin' bout rights, de white men will be in a fix pretty soon … Dat man ober dar say dat women needs to be helped into carriages, and lifted ober ditches, and to have de best place everywhere. Nobody eber helped me into carriages, or ober mud puddles, or give me any best place. And ain't I a Woman?
>
> (Truth 104)

During her lifetime as a staunch upholder of truth and justice, Sojourner Truth, born a slave in 1797 and freed under the 1827 New York State Emancipation Act, often unexpectedly appeared at antislavery and women's rights rallies. Her impromptu remarks often refuted antagonistic arguments against both her race and her sex, and in that order. Her frequently quoted speech above, which was both unsolicited and initially unwelcomed because of her color by the White audience at an 1852 Women's Rights Convention in Akron, Ohio, is used here to demonstrate the critical position of the Africana woman within the context of the modern feminist movement.

Historically, Africana women have fought against sexual discrimination as well as race and class discrimination. They have challenged Africana male chauvinism but have stopped short of eliminating Africana men as allies in the struggle for liberation and familyhood. Historically, Africana women have wanted to be "liberated" to the community, family, and its responsibilities. The daily evacuation of males and females from the Africana community in a nine-to-five society has wreaked havoc on the sense of security of Africana children. The distress of these Africana children and their need for comforting seems to have been ignored, overlooked, and vastly underplayed, suggesting that these children do not need this kind of support. The result is generations of hurt and rejection. Even Africana women who happen to be on welfare and may be at home are condemned for not having a job and are, thus, often not regarded as positive figures for these children, even though they at least offer an adult presence. With polarized minds, Africanan have bought into

DOI: 10.4324/9781032720036-4

this view, embracing all too frequently the stereotype of the Africana woman on welfare and society's disapproval of them. Nevertheless, Africana women are seeking to reclaim security, stability, and nurturing of a family-based community.

According to Africana sociologist Vivian Gordon in *Black Women, Feminism and Black Liberation: Which Way*?

> To address women's issues, therefore, is not only to address the crucial needs of Black women, it is also to address the historic primacy of the African and African American community; that is, the primacy of its children and their preparation for the responsibilities and privileges of mature personhood.
>
> (viii)

Africana women have historically demonstrated that they are diametrically opposed to the concept of many White feminists who want independence and freedom from family responsibility. In the Statement of Purpose, which was issued by the National Organization of Women **(NOW)** in 1966 and which is still in effect today, "it is no longer either necessary or possible for women to devote the greater part of their lives to child rearing."[2] Some women take this statement a step further and wish to be liberated not only from their families but from their obligation to men in particular. This sentiment may appeal more to radical lesbian feminists or radical feminist separatists. Many White feminists deny traditional familyhood as an integral part of their personal and professional lives.

All too frequently, Sojourner's resounding query "And ain't I a woman?" is extrapolated from the text in order to force a feminist identification of the speaker without any initial or even later reference to her first obstacle, which is her race. As mentioned earlier, during Sojourner's speech in 1852, Whites had not even deemed her as human, let alone deemed her as a woman, which is precisely why she was mocked before they finally allowed her to speak. One may question what this has to do with the modern feminist movement. The fact is that these racist perceptions have not changed significantly as to suggest that Africana women do not yet have to contend with the same problem of insidious racism, with almost equal intensity even though it is somewhat masked today.

In attempting to unearth the historical truths about the feminist movement that divide the White feminist from Africana women, Africana literary theorist Hazel V. Carby asserts: "In order to gain a public voice as orators or published writers, black women had to confront the dominant domestic ideologies and literary conventions of woman-hood which excluded them from the definition 'women'" (6). Moreover, many White feminists have ironically used Sojourner's quotation to justify labeling this freedom fighter as a feminist or a "pre-feminist." Often, they include their interpretation of the Africana experience and when it is convenient Sojourner's experience becomes a dramatization of female oppression. Ironically, Sojourner was not embracing the Women's Rights Movement; instead, she was attacking that element of the Women's Rights agenda that excluded her. Instead of establishing a feminist alignment, she was engaging in self-actualization, forcing White women in particular to recognize her and all Africana women as women, and as a definite and legitimate part of society in general. During the abolitionist movement White women learned from Africana women techniques on how to organize, hold public meetings, and conduct petition campaigns. As abolitionists, the White women first learned to speak in public and began to develop a philosophy of their place in society and of their basic rights. Africana women, on the other hand, learned and practiced all these same things centuries ago in their ancestral home of Africa.

Procrusteans have mislabeled Africana women activists, like Sojourner Truth, and other prominent Africana women freedom fighters, such as Harriet Tubman and Ida B. Wells, simply because they were women. Indeed, the primary concerns of these women were not of a feminist nature, but rather a commitment to the centrality of the African American freedom struggle. Their primary concern was the life-threatening plight of all Africana people, both men and women, at the hands of a racist system. To cast them in a feminist mode, which de-emphasizes their major interest, is an abomination and an outright insult to their level of struggle.

Too many Blacks have taken the theoretical framework of "feminism" and have tried to make it fit their particular circumstance. Rather than create their own paradigm and name and define themselves, some Africana women, scholars in particular, have been persuaded by White feminists to adopt or to adapt to the White concept and terminology of feminism. The real benefit of the amalgamation of Black feminism and White feminism goes to White feminists who can increase their power base by expanding their scope with the convenient consensus that sexism is their commonality and primary concern. They make a gender analysis of Africana-American life with the goal of equating racism with sexism. Politically and ideologically for Africana women, such an adoption is misguided and simplistic. Most Africanans do not share the same ideology as traditional White feminists. True, the two groups may share strategies for ending sexual discrimination, but they are divided on how to change the entire political system to end racial discrimination and sexual exploitation. While the White feminist has not sacrificed her major concern, sexism, the Black feminist has, in that she has yielded to her primary concern for racism and is forced to see classism as secondary and tertiary issues. The modified terminology, "Black Feminism," is some Africana women's futile attempt to fit into the constructs of an established White female paradigm. At best, Black feminism may relate to sexual discrimination outside of the Africana community but cannot claim to resolve the critical problems within it, which are influenced by racism and classism.

White feminist Bettina Aptheker, daughter of Harvard University history professor, Dr. Herbert Aptheker, accurately analyzes the problem:

> When we place women at the center of our thinking, we are going about the business of creating an historical and cultural matrix from which women may claim autonomy and independence over their own lives. For women of color, such autonomy cannot be achieved in conditions of racial oppression and cultural genocide … In short, "feminist," in the modern sense, means the empowerment of women. For women of color, such an equality, such an empowerment, cannot take place unless the communities in which they live can successfully establish their own racial and cultural integrity. (Aptheker 13)

For many White women, Africana women exist for their purpose—a dramatization of oppression. As for their identity, they consider themselves the definitive woman and thus there is no need, for example, to name their studies "White" Women's Studies. Moreover, while gender-specific discrimination is the key issue for Women's Studies, it unfortunately narrows the goals of Africana liberation and devalues the quality of Africana life. Gender-specific neither identifies nor defines the primary issue for Africana women or other non-White women. It is crucial that Africana women engage in self-naming and self-definition, lest they fall into the trap of refining a critical ideology at the risk of surrendering the sense of identity.

Africana women might begin by naming and defining their unique movement "Africana Womanism." The concept of Womanism can be traced back to Sojourner's speech that began to develop and highlight Africana women's unique experience into a paradigm for Africana women. In refining this terminology into a theoretical framework and methodology, "Africana Womanism" identifies the participation and the role of Africana women in the struggle but does not suggest that female subjugation is the most critical issue they face in their struggle for parity. Like Black feminism, Africana Womanism acknowledges societal gender problems as critical issues to be resolved; however, it views feminism, the suggested alternative to these problems, as a sort of inverted White patriarchy, with the White feminist now in command and on top. Mainstream feminism is women's co-opting themselves into mainstream patriarchal values. According to Gordon, "The Movement fails to state clearly that the system is wrong; what it does communicate is that White women want to be a part of the system. They seek power, not change" (47).

The Africana womanist, on the other hand, perceives herself as the companion to the Africana man, and works diligently toward continuing their established union in the struggle against racial oppression. Within the Africana culture, there is an intrinsic, organic equality that has always been necessary for the survival of the Africana culture, in spite of the individual personal problems of female subjugation that penetrated the Africana family structure as a result of the White male cultural system. This issue must be addressed. However, the White male's privilege is not the Africana men's or women's personal problem but rather a political problem of unchallenged gender chauvinism in the world. Critiquing Women's Studies, Aptheker concludes that:

> women's studies programs operate within a racist structure. Every department in every predominantly white institution is centered on the experience, history, politics, and culture of white men, usually of the elite. What is significant, however, is that women's studies, by its very reason for existence, implies a reordering of politics, a commitment to community, and an educational purpose which is inherently subversive of its institutional setting … Insofar as women's studies replicates a racial pattern in which white rule predominates, however, it violates its own principles of origin and purpose. More to the point: it makes impossible the creation of a feminist vision and politics.
>
> (13)

Africanans have critical and complex problems in their community, most of which stem from racial oppression. The Africana woman acknowledges the problem of classism, a reproachable· element in America's capitalistic system. However, even there the plight of the middle-class Africana woman becomes intertwined with racism. Given that both the Africana womanist and the Black feminist address these critical issues and more, there must be something that makes the issues of the Africana womanist different, and that something is prioritizing on the part of the Africana woman. She realizes the critical need to prioritize the antagonistic forces as racism, classism, and sexism, respectively. In the final analysis, Africana Womanism is connected to the tradition of self-reliance and autonomy, working toward participation in Africana liberation.

Observe the importance of Africana identity in the case of Sojourner Truth, for example. Before one can properly address her much-quoted query, one must, as she did, first consider her color, for it was because of color that Sojourner was initially hissed and jeered at for having the gall to address the conflict between men and women and the rights of the latter. Before Sojourner could hope to address gender problems, she had to first overcome discrimination from her White audience. Clearly, gender was not her primary concern. By reiterating "And Ain't I a Woman," Sojourner insisted that she, too, possessed all the traits of a woman, notwithstanding her race and class, that the dominant culture used to exclude her from that community. The key issue for the Africana woman, as well as for the Africana man, is racism, with classism intertwined therein.

While women of all ethnic orientations share the unfortunate commonality of female subjugation, it is naive, to say the least, to suggest that this kind of oppression should be the primary concern of all women, particularly women of color. When the Black feminist buys the White terminology, she also buys its agenda. Because Africana women share other forms of oppression that are not necessarily a part of the overall White women's experiences, their varied kinds of victimization need to be prioritized. Instead of alienating the Africana male sector from the struggle today, Africanans must call for a renegotiation of Africana male-female roles in society. In so doing, there must be a call to halt once and for all female subjugation, while continuing the critical struggle for the liberation of Africana people worldwide.

As previously stated, the notion of Africana women moving "from margin to center"[3] of the feminist movement, as proposed· by bell hooks, is ludicrous, for how can any woman hope to move from the peripheral to the center of a movement that, historically, has not included her on the agenda. Even during the resurgence of the Women's Liberation Movement of the mid-1960s the critical concerns of the Africana woman were not part of the agenda. Be that as it may, Hooks complains that contemporary Africana women do not join together for women's rights because they do not see womanhood as an important aspect of their identity. Further, she states that racist and sexist socialization have conditioned Africana women to devalue their femaleness and to regard race as their only relevant label of identity. In short, she surmises that Africana women have been asked to deny a part of themselves and they have. Clearly, this position evokes some controversy, as it does not take into account the reasons for the Africana woman's reluctance to embrace feminism.

Consider the experience of a woman who said that from so many feet away, her race was noticed; as she got into closer proximity, her class was detected; but that it was not until she got in the door that her sex was known. Does that not suggest the need for prioritizing? The prioritizing of the kinds of relegation to which the Africana woman is subjected should be explored in a serious effort to recognize and to understand the existence of her total sense of oppression. What one really wants to do is appreciate the triple plight of Africana women. Society needs to deal with all aspects of the oppression of the Africana woman in order to better combat them. Race and class biases are the key issues for non-Whites and must be resolved even before gender issues if there is any hope for human survival. It is impossible to conceive of any human being succumbing to absolute regression without an outright struggle against it.

Sojourner Truth demonstrated early on in the Women's Rights Movement that a commonality exists between the Africana men and women of the South and the women of the North in their struggle for freedom. Clearly, the Africana woman had, neither then nor now, no exclusive claim on the struggle for equal rights apart from her male counterpart. Africana men and Africana women are and should be allies, struggling as they have since the days of slavery for equal social, economic, and political rights as fellow human beings in the world. There is an inherent contradiction in the ideology of "Black Feminism" that should be reevaluated. A more compatible concept is "Africana Womanism." Indeed, this issue must be properly addressed if Black Women in the struggle for total parity are to be truly respected and, moreover, if a positive agenda for Africana Women is to be truly realized.

Notes

1 This chapter is reprinted with permission from *The Western Journal of Black Studies,* which first appeared in the Winter 1989 issue. The author introduced the "Africana Womanism" concept at the National Council for Black Studies Conference, March 1986.

2 NOW Statement of Purpose (adopted at the organizing conference in Washington, DC, October 29, 1966).

3 See bell hooks' Feminist *Theory: From Margin to Center.*

3 The 18 Descriptors of the Africana Womanist

> The fact of the matter is that Africana Womanism is a response to the need for collective definition and the re-creation of the authentic agenda that is the birthright of every living person.
>
> (Asante, Afterword, *Africana Womanist* 138)

It is the responsibility of all Africana women to name and define themselves, as implied in the above quotation, and this chapter attempts to do just that, lest we fall victim to being misnamed and ill-defined by others. There are many positive characteristics of a true Africana womanist, but there are 18 distinct features, as I have observed them time and again, which accurately describe our basic nature and actions for centuries, dating back to antiquity. They are self-namer, self-definer, family-centered, genuine in sisterhood, strong, in concert with male in struggle, whole, authentic, flexible role player, respected, recognized, spiritual, male-compatible, respectful of elders, adaptable, ambitious, and mother and nurturing.

As the old saying goes, there is nothing new in the universe. Well, that is true also of the Africana woman, as modern-day Africana women continue, though oftentimes unconsciously so, the rich legacy of African womanhood. In her article entitled "Africana Womanism—An African Legacy: It Ain't Easy Being a Queen," anthropologist, Dr. Barbara Wheeler

> make[s] some observations about the world-wide institutions of marriage and family. The conclusion contains thoughts regarding the visible legacy of ancient African queens, queen warriors, and ordinary African women, and their impact upon contemporary women of African heritage…. It has now been acknowledged that humankind originated in Africa; that is, that the continent of Africa is the cradle of humanity. We also know that the hand that rocks the cradle historically has been the hand of a woman, the culture bearer. It is for this reason that we must laud Lewis, Mary, and Richard Leakey for resurrecting the oldest known African queen. In 1962, from the diggings of Olduvai Gorge, in Tanzania, the Leakeys unearthed

DOI: 10.4324/9781032720036-5

> the fossil that helped establish that humans, as we know them today, did originate in Africa.
>
> (*Contemporary Africana Theory* 320 & 321)

That said, I will now define the Africana womanist's 18 descriptors, with a rhymed couplet underneath each, which she convincingly embodies to a varying degree:

Self-Namer
I chose my name; we choose; it's all our business.
Stay in your lane; agree—an uncontested "yes."

Nommo, a term used in African cosmology to indicate naming, is critical. In fact, Barbara Christian, a major literary critic in the field of Africana literature, asserts that "it is through *nommo*, the correct naming of a thing that it comes into existence" (Christian 157–158). The Africana woman, in realizing and properly accessing herself and her movement, must, then, properly name herself and her movement, Africana womanist and Africana Womanism, respectively, which even Christian herself fails to do, as well as many other women of African descent. Moreover, Filomina Chioma Steady, a well-known Africana critic, in her introduction to *The Black Woman Cross-Culturally*, is another example of this via the misnaming issue, as she mistakenly names African women the "original feminist," though her analysis of the historical and current role and activity of the Africana woman is accurate:

> True feminism springs from an actual experience of oppression, a lack of the socially prescribed means of ensuring one's well-being, and a true lack of access to resources for survival. True feminism is the reaction which leads to the development of greater resourcefulness for survival and greater self-reliance. Above all, true feminism is impossible without intensive involvement in production. All over the African Diaspora, but particularly on the continent, the black woman's role in this regard is paramount. It can, therefore, be stated with much justification that the black woman is to a large extent the original feminist.
>
> (36)

Is she not aware that history reveals that the practice of the feminist was that of racism, which is oppression personified? Thus, all that the Africana woman is and has been does not make her a feminist, a concept that evolved long after her beginnings in Africa and, more important, does not protect the humanity of the Africana woman. To be sure, the Africana womanist is her own person, operating according to the forces in her life, and thus her name must reflect true authenticity, which starts with proper naming.

Always a self-namer, even during American slavery when the White slave owners of the slave woman labeled her as a breeder for American society, the Africana womanist insisted upon identifying herself as mother and companion. Even though her children and her spouse were often taken from her, a common slave phenomenon, she did not relinquish her identity, and, thus, a grieving mother and companion, she often held to the memories of her family. She knew that regardless of how the dominant culture viewed her, her "humanness" contradicted their naming of her. As Sojourner says in her famous 1851 oration, interestingly at a white women's convention, to which she was not welcomed, "I have born'd five children and seen 'em mos' all sold off into slavery, and when I cried out with mother's grief, none but Jesus heard and ain't I a woman?" (Truth, 104). Despite all, she was a woman and a mother, not mere property, and, thus, Whites could neither control nor dictate her knowledge of these factors nor her natural human response to them.

Self-Definer
The definition of who I really "be,"
Will make it crystal clear for all to see.

Self-defining must follow self-defining, as the Africana womanist must ensure consistency in her total being and identity. Nobel laureate Toni Morrison says it well in her Pulitzer Prize-winning novel, *Beloved*, wherein the narrator asserts that "Definitions belonged to the definers—not the defined" (190). That was, of course, during slavery, even though noted historian Dr. John Blassingame, in his classic history of the true lives of the enslaved, *The Slave Community: Plantation Life in the Antebellum South*, presents the African American slaves, women in particular, as Africana womanists, who have always conducted themselves as members of a collective community, maintaining the African ways of being. This means that we are one, operating in concert with one another, men and women, which contradicts, in a real sense, the notion of the other defining who we really are. Thus,

> We as Africana people must decide for ourselves who we are and what our agenda need be. Africana people must engage in identifying our own demands, beginning with self-naming and self-definition, so that we can better focus on what it will take for us to realize total human parity.
> (Hudson (Weems), *"Self-Naming and Self-Definition"* 451)

Hence, despite the superficial definitions assigned to us by the dominant culture, we are family; we love and cherish each other.

Family-Centered
You, me, and they—family centrality—
That's what it means to us; it's our reality.

A chief feature of the Africana womanist is her family-centeredness. It is her entire family, not just the female component, with whom the Africana womanist concerns herself. She is ever mindful of the fact that we are "in it together." On the other hand, the traditional mainstream feminist takes a position of female centrality, emphasizing the concerns of the female more than the concerns of the entire family, including the male counterpart, the decided position of the Africana Womanist:

> ...Family centrality—That's it; we're going nowhere without the other.
> That means the men, the women, and children, too
> Truly collectively working—"I got your back, Boo."
> (Hudson (Weems), *"I Got Your Back, Boo,"* 2009)

> Although for some in general, to some degree, that has changed, while great emphasis is still being placed on the concerns for female empowerment.

> *Strong*
> *It's more than just one way to show true power.*
> *Morning, noon, or night, no matter the hour.*

Generally speaking, the Africana womanist comes from a long tradition of spiritual, psychological, as well as physical strength. For centuries, she and her family have struggled for ultimate survival. But at the same time, we have had to witness our male counterparts' powerlessness, suffering the inability to fulfill their traditional, God-given role as protector and provider. Thus, the Africana womanist

> ...is not expected to abandon them or badger them with the too-frequent generalization that all Africana men are no good or irredeemable. Such a personal self-serving mis-labeling inevitably ends in an unjustifiable and relentless lashing out at men in general, thereby sentencing them to perpetual verbal and emotional castration by their women.
> (Hudson (Weems), *Africana Womanism* 51–52)

Yes, the Africana Womanist is strong, but it's far more than mere physical strength. It's emotional, psychological, and spiritual, too, that powerful inner strength that enables her to demonstrate love for her entire family.

> *In Concert with Males in Struggle*
> *It takes "two to tango" to be a winner.*
> *And then celebrate with a marvelous dinner.*

The Africana womanist is also in concert with males in the broader struggle for humanity and the liberation of all Africana people. The very idea of the intertwined destiny of Africana men, women, and children is directly related to the notion of the dependency upon the male sector in the participation of the Africana womanist's struggle for herself and her family. The struggle of the mainstream feminist, on the other hand, does not encourage male participation; however, the Africana womanist does, as she invites her male counterpart into her struggle for liberation on all fronts, thereby making survival possible, at least to some degree, in a very hostile and racist society. Granted, Africana women and white women do share some critical gender issues, but how to resolve the issues should not rest upon excluding the very instrument of female subjugation, which is the male. This is extremely problematic for Africana people, as we cannot afford the gender divide. According to sociologist Dr. Mark Christian, in the Afterword in *Africana Womanism*,

> This [prioritization of race, class and gender] by no means weakens the analysis of empowerment for Africana women, for it actually strengthens the analysis away from dividing Africana women from their men, whether it be spouses, brothers, nephews, cousins, uncles, fathers, and so. We need Africana womanism more than ever because the insidious divide and conquer tactics found in many female-based constructs is playing a key role in the demise of Africana communities. All things stated the Africana world is under tremendous assault. We need to take firm responsibility for this and that means individual and collective, men and women. Clenora Hudson (Weems), pulls no punches. She is more than astute to the fact that women are at the center of most things in the Africana world. However, there is no need to denigrate and weaken further the overall spirit of Black men.
>
> (Christian 131 & 151)

Genuine Sisterhood
Girlfriend, you feel me, and that's for real.
My woes and my joys are also your deal.

The beautiful bounding among Africana women—Genuine Sisterhood—has always been in existence and that bonding cannot be easily broken. And the beauty of it all is that it is reciprocal, wherein each gives and receives equally. Collectively, they embrace each other, feeling both their pain and their joys in sharing each other's experiences, which is given out of a genuine love and respect for each other.

It goes without saying that there is no substitute for genuine sisterhood, which is an asexual relationship between women, for there will always be a need for women to connect for support and guidance during those times when words of encouragement are most needed. Such friendships are, indeed, invaluable, and, thus, with such love and trust, it is difficult to imagine life without genuine sisterhood.

Flexible Role Players
When you're here, you do you, I do me, we're one.
When you are not, I switch roles, I do what must be done.

Another characteristic of the Africana womanist is that of flexible role player. This is a controversial topic today, grounded in the historical predicament of the Africana man and woman, which dates back to American slavery, during which time neither was free to act out the defined roles of the sexes as set forth by the dominant culture. For example, the Africana woman has never been restricted to the home, which has been oftentimes shared by her male counterpart, resulting from racist job discrimination prohibiting employment for many men. "Last hired; first fired."

According to Sara Evans, the roles in the Africana community have always been nearly indistinguishable. For example, Africana women have not had the long-standing role as "only" homemaker, a traditional role from which White women look forward to retiring:

> Certain differences result from the way in which Black women grow up. We have been raised to function independently. The notion of retiring to housewifery someday is not even a reasonable fantasy. Therefore, whether you want to or not, it is necessary to learn to do all of the things required to do to survive. It seemed to many of us, on the other hand, that white women were demanding a chance to be independent while we needed help and assistance that was not always forth coming. We definitely started from opposite ends of the spectrum.
>
> …we did the same work as men … usually with men.
>
> (239–240)

Moreover, Africana men likewise have not consistently experienced the fulfillment of their role as head of the household, a position traditionally expected of men. Today, that tradition is being dismantled by the mainstream feminist, whereas the Africana womanist accepts many traditional roles, as many are valid, as there are some biological distinctions between the sexes. Let it be known that although Africana women uphold traditional roles in general, those roles have long been somewhat relaxed in the Black community.

Male Compatible
I got your back, Boo, you got mine;
It's like having the best of red or white wine.

The Africana womanist desires a positive male relationship, one in which everyone is mutually supportive, which is very much a part of the positive

Africana family. In the Africana community, neither women nor men can afford to conclude that the other gender is irredeemable, hence undesirable. Such a stance of totally disregarding or dismissing the other could resort in racial suicide. Note that during the experiences of strong Africana women being abandoned by men, there are millions of Africana women with entirely different experiences. While they praised their hardworking husbands and fathers, they got little or no recognition for their acts. Too often, such stories/cases have been somehow overlooked. To be sure, positive male companionship is an aspiration for the average Africana womanist, for she realizes that male and female relationships are not only comforting but key to perpetuating humanity, without which humanity becomes extinct.

The Africana womanist also realizes that, while she loves and respects herself and is, in general, at peace with herself, she ultimately desires a special somebody to fill a void in her life, one who makes her complete. Terry McMillan considers the desires of many Africana women for positive male companionship and comments on the void in many of their lives in many of her novels:

> We don't have a husband or a steady man in our lives, though most of us would like to … We spend too many precious hours on the phone, over dinner—everywhere —discussing the problems and perils of wanting, loving and needing black men.
>
> (McMillan, *"Hers"*)

The reality is that the riff between men and women, traditionally called "the battle of the sexes," is that Africana men and women have shared experiences and responsibilities. In other words, they have much in common. However, while they are in search of positive male/female relationships, they are not interested in just merely settling for companionship for the sake of having a man, which is the farthest thing from the best-case scenario of the true Africana womanist.

Spiritual
God the Father, our spirituality—
Jesus completes this thing; it's true reality.

The Africana womanist demonstrates a strong sense of spirituality, which is a belief in a higher power that transcends limitations of the physical world. Acknowledging the existence of spiritual reality brings into play the power in accepting the inexplicable, and the power of God's healing. It is a natural phenomenon in the traditional lives of Africana people, which has been and continues to be handed down from generation to generation, and thus spirituality must be included in the character of Africana women. In almost every aspect of the Africana womanist's life, she bears witness to this aspect of African cosmology, whether it is consciously or subconsciously executed.

In observing the Africana woman in making everyday decisions, one senses her reliance upon the inner spirit or mind, trusting in God for answers. And in health care, she frequently goes back to folk medicine and spiritual healing, including the laying on of hands, which entails placing hands on others while praying for a healing. Indeed, in being connected to the spiritual world, with undaunted faith, she is invariably guided spiritually by God. Indeed, in African cosmology, the physical and spiritual worlds co-exist and hence both realities complement each other in working for the good of all who believe in and trust in God.

Whole
I am complete, a full-fledge human being,
Not one dimensional but endowed with God's gift of seeing.

The true Africana womanist seeks wholeness (completeness). Understandably, by now she wants it all, or at least as much as she can secure. That means she wants her home, her family, and her career, neglecting none. Granted, the family does come first in the priorities of Africana women, but other things, too, are very important, as they come together, ensuring both harmony and security in the home for all to enjoy.

In acquiring wholeness, the Africana womanist also demonstrates her desire for a positive male companionship, for without her male counterpart, her life is not complete in a real sense. She needs male companionship and, likewise, he needs female companionship, for, in the final analysis, both are essential to the survival of the human race. Her sense of wholeness is necessarily compatible with her cultural consciousness and authentic existence.

Authentic
I'm Black and Beautiful and very proud of it.
I love my roots and my family—every little bit.

As an authentic being, authenticity (cultural connection) in her life, her standards, her acts, and her ideals directly reflect those dictated by her own culture. Hence, her true essence complements her culture, thereby denying any room for an inauthentic self. Collectively, wholeness and authenticity are powerful tenets of the Africana womanist. Her heritage strongly stresses the importance of the family unit.

Respectful of Elders
Why disrespect the ones who came before?
They made your life a fuller one, with much more.

The true African womanist has great respect and appreciation of her elders, and, therefore, she insists that her children, too, revere them. Having paved the way for us, elders served as our true role models. This respect and appreciation for them is yet another African cultural continuum, for the true Africana woman continues to show this respect for elders daily. Moreover, she naturally protects them and seeks their advice as well. As evidenced, the elders' blessed years of experience have afforded them awesome wisdom. As a result, they are a seminal part of the Africana family, deserving of all our love and respect. One has to wonder, then, about the salient question: Where would we be without our elders?

Respected
I expect respect, which I surely deserved.
I returned to you the same, and not unnerved.

Above all, the Africana womanist expects her male companion to respect her as a first step toward appreciating and respecting both himself and others. If there is a lack of self-love, which naturally evolves into self-hate, then there is no room for truly loving anyone else. For example, this lack of having respect for self, represented accepting the White standard of beauty, is the center of what Toni Morrison discusses in *The Bluest Eye*, wherein the main character is depicted as having a negative sense of herself, in terms of her beauty, or lack thereof.[1] But it goes further. What ultimately happens in the lives of many is having an absolute "zero image" of oneself.[2] This could possibly result in allowing oneself to be disrespected, abused, and trampled on by anybody, including the male. Hence, the gender factor is important for the Africana family as well. Therefore, the Africana woman must continue to seek feasible ways of combating this triple problem within her own community. Whether it is a problem of race, class, or sex, the Africana woman must first have respect for her own personhood, which would naturally flow over to expecting respect from others as well.

Recognized
I am not invisible, as surely you can see.
I see you, you see me, as well as it should be.

The true Africana Womanist also desires recognition of her personhood, her humanness, in order that she may more effectively fulfill her role as a positive and responsible companion in the overall Africana family/structure. The Africana man, too, must do his part, beginning with recognition of his female counterpart. In short, recognizing, as well as respecting, each other, is truly a reciprocal thing that must be an integral part of our lives.

Adaptable
Whatever is needed, I'll make it happen now.
I promise I will, for sure, and you have my vow.

The true Africana womanist demands no separate space for nourishing her individual needs and goals, while in the twentieth-century feminist movement, there is the White feminist's insistence upon personal space. One of the leading mainstream feminists, Virginia Woolf, insists that women must have their separate space, preferably a place away from home, for them to be truly creative.[3] A woman must have, she feels, a room of her own, a place to escape to, for success and creativity. This could allow the intellectual freedom that depends upon material things, which comments upon the necessity of economic freedom. A separate space for most Africana women, as well as for lower-working-class women in general, is not only impossible but inconceivable. These women in general often have limited funds. Taking those funds to defray expenses for a separate space, which necessarily means renting a place and hiring a sitter for the children in most cases, would in effect mean taking the necessities from the family. Needless to say, this is not the common reality of Africana woman. However, the absence of a separate space does not render her non-creative; neither does it render her unsuccessful.

Ambitious
My quest is motivated by love of life;
God promised us happiness, without the strife.

Ambition and responsibility are highly important in the life of the Africana womanist, for her family, too, depends on these qualities in her. From early on, the Africana woman is taught the importance of self-reliance and resourcefulness, and, hence, she makes a way out of no way, creating ways to realize her goals and objectives in life. The sense of responsibility she has for her family is paramount and so she creates a private space for herself during chaos, confusion, and congestion, even while washing dishes, feeding the baby, or cooking dinner. It may be in a tiny room, or a closet, or it may be in the wee hours after bedtime for her family, but not a totally separate space away from her family. Whatever the case, the Africana woman, with ingenuity, provides herself with whatever is necessary for her creative energies to soar. Thus, within the walls of some Africana homes lurk many perceptive and creative Africana women writers, for example, workers, without rooms of their own, who explore their myriad experiences in attempts to create some artistic semblance of their realities, perspectives, and possibilities regarding the status of the Africana community—its women, its men, and its children. In the final analysis, the Africana womanist is her own person, fully equipped with her own problems, her own successes, her own set of priorities.

Mothering and Nurturing
A mother's love for her children ensures a healthy body, mind, soul.
Her labor for each of them is equivalent to precious gold.

Finally, the Africana womanist is committed to the art of mothering and nurturing her own children and humankind in general. This collective role is supreme in Africana culture, for the Africana woman comes from a legacy of fulfilling the role of supreme Mother Nature—nurturer, provider, and protector. Historically, the role of mother was more important than the role of wife, for example, as the Africana woman operates from within these constructs. Unlike many White feminists quoted in Davidson's *The Failure of Feminism*, such as Kate Millet (who calls for the abolition of the traditional role of the mother), Germaine Greer (who expounds upon the crucial plight of mothers), Betty Rollin (who contends that motherhood is none other than a concept adopted from society by women), and Betty Friedan (who pleads the case of pathology in children of careerless, overprotective mothers), the Africana womanist comes from a legacy of dedicated wives and mothers. And, thus, according to Algea Harrison:

> Black women have consistently indicated that they value the role of mother and consider it an important aspect of their sex role identity. Indeed, there was evidence that Black women sometimes prioritized the mother role over wife and worker roles.
>
> (204)

Enjoying her role, she both encourages her own and sacrifices herself in executing her duty to humanity. In molding character, she will ensure that her children will grow up to continue the legacy that she has set forth—doing what must be done for the survival of the family.

In conclusion, the key descriptors of the true Africana/Africana-Melanated Womanist are very important, as they bring forth a holistic existence for both her and her family. Refining a paradigm relative to who the Africana womanist is and has always been could conceivably enable us to better resolve the existing conflict between Africana women and particularly the gap characterizing modern-day male/female relationships. Once this is resolved, we could witness a beautiful union between the genders that would inevitably bring about a harmonious world for all—men, women, and children. And "To God Be the Glory."

Notes

1 Toni Morrison's *The Bluest Eye* offers further insights into the devastating impact of buying into an alien standard of beauty. An analysis of this is in Chapter 2—"The Damaging Look: The Search for Authentic Existence in *The Bluest Eye*"—in Wilfred Samuels and Clenora Hudson (Weems)' *Toni Morrison* (1990).

2 The "zero image" is a term coined by Carolyn Gerald in "The Black Writer and His Role" in Addison Gayle's *The Black Aesthetics*.

3 For further discussion on Virginia Woolf 's theory of "separate space," see her book entitled *A Room of One's Own* (1957).

4 The Africana Womanist Male Counterpart

> It is fairly difficult to finalize the dynamics of the true Africana woman without giving some attention to her male counterpart, the positive Africana man. It seems only plausible and natural that the Africana man would have characteristics commensurate with those of *his* counterpart. Thus, in observing positive Africana men, it becomes clear that positive Africana men share similar qualities with the Africana woman.
>
> (*Africana Womanism First Edition* 144)

From this quotation, coming from the Conclusion in the First Edition of the 1993 publication, *Africana Womanism: Reclaiming Ourselves*, it should be clear that the male, be he the father, the husband or significant other, the son, the sibling, or the friend, and the list continues, it is crystal clear that the male and the female are inextricably connected. Logically, it's virtually impossible to be anti-male, or anti-anybody for that matter, for we are fellow human beings. But for now, we'll focus on the Africana male, the counterpart for the Africana woman, for a better sense of his overall make-up, both inside and outside, as our lives are, indeed, interconnected. Just as I have enumerated and expounded upon the 18 characteristics of the true Africana woman, I must here likewise enumerate and define the 18 characteristics of the true Africana man:

Self-Namer
I'm not the beta man you say I am.
I hold my family as my own program.

Like the Africana woman, the Africana man must insist upon naming himself, never allowing others to name him, for then, you would be giving them power over your life, your domain, and your destiny. Whenever someone takes the liberty of assigning your identity to you, without your permission, your responsibility is to reject it by claiming that privilege yourself. For example, too often are men called "dogs" by women who feel that in some way or another, they have been mistreated or disrespected by them. The connotation

DOI: 10.4324/9781032720036-6

of such a term is loaded with negative meanings, such as low down and dirty, promiscuous, violent, and uncaring. For the most part, dogs are quite the opposite of what is inferred. For centuries they have been called "Man's best friend," as they have proven to be loyal, protective, faithful, and very affectionate. When others would abandon you, they would be there, right by your side. Thus, one must be careful in trusting others in the serious act of naming. It is a responsibility that you must insist upon, or you may become what that name otherwise has come to represent.

Self-Definer
Define me as of no significance,
Is next to telling me I have no pants.

As critical to self-naming is self-defining, as they are inextricably linked together. Names and definitions are very difficult to separate, though terminology and meaning could have a slight difference. For example, a respected French linguist, Ferdinand de Saussure comments on the dynamics of language, which he contends do not convey reality. He asserts that language is a system of signs (words) and that inherent are both signifiers (signs/words) and the signified (the actual thing itself, regardless of the term assigned to it). Thus, assigning a word to a thing does not create that which the word suggests. As the old saying goes, "A rose by any other name is still a rose." That said, we must be careful with the matter of definitions to ensure accuracy.

Family-Centered
My family is the center of my world.
We stand together, no matter what the peril.

The true Africana man must be family-centered, as his family should be his number one priority. The man, generally referred to as the head of the household, must assume the responsibility of the safety and security of his family. His family depends upon him for guidance and strength, but it is important to know and understand that his female counterpart has the responsibility to share those family concerns with him. As his co-partner, she must be by his side to uphold those things necessary for the survival of their family, realizing that together they can make almost anything happen. Senegalese writer Mariama Bâ makes an excellent case of family centrality in her novel *So Long a Letter*:

> I remain persuaded of the inevitable and necessary complementarity of man and woman.
>
> Love, imperfect as it may be in its content and expression, remains the natural link between these two beings.
>
> To love one another! If only each partner could move sincerely towards the other! If each could only melt into the other! If each would only accept the

> other's successes and failures! If each would only praise the other's qualities instead of listing his faults! If each could only correct bad habits without harping on about them! If each could penetrate the other's most secret haunts to forestall failure and be a support while tending to the evils that are repressed!
>
> The success of the family is born of a couple's harmony, as the harmony of multiple instruments creates a pleasant symphony.
>
> The nation is made up of all the families, rich and poor, united or separated, aware or unaware. The success of a nation therefore depends inevitably on the family.
>
> (88–89)

And so you have it, family centrality in a nutshell!

Role Model
I proudly stand as exemplar for manhood—
The husband, the father, and everything good, I possibly could.

Good role models are very important to any group. They stand as examples of how we must be, how we think, and how we act. For the Africana man, he must represent the positive of which the woman is proud and to which the children can aspire. In short, he should be someone whom all should be proud to have as a part of their lives. For example, in Toni Morrison's *Beloved*, Sethe, Paul D. represents that special one, indeed, the supreme example of a positive male role model. He cares for not only his woman, but her family as well, and wants only the best for her, always insisting that "You your best thing, Sethe. You are" (Morrison 273).

Strong
I use my strength to protect my family—
My wife, my children, my all—just let us be.

Traditionally, the man represents the physical strength of the family. But like the Africana woman, he must have both physical and emotional strength. While it is expected of him to use his physical prowess, to move an object, for example, it is not to be misused, such as to inflict violence on his female counterpart. When a man does this, he has violated the physical power God has given him for other purposes. If guilty of such perverse and cowardly acts, he can be assured that in time, he will experience retribution and/or abandonment in one form or another. The Africana man must be strong and sure of himself, and not succumb to abusing his mate to make himself look stronger.

Committed to Struggle
No matter what, I embrace our common mission—
Ensuring our people to bring forth the vision.

The concerted efforts of the Africana man and woman are critical to our liberation struggle. Nothing could be more rewarding than the coming together of these two entities in working toward the success, happiness, and overall well-being of the family and the community. This feature of the Africana man is further expounded upon in Chapter 6 of *Africana Womanism*, "Africana Male-Female Relationships and Sexism in the Africana Community."

Whole
I'm far more than a mere surface figure;
Indeed, my scope is big and getting bigger.

Being a complete person, whole and well-rounded, is essential to love and happiness. The Africana man needs this quality in order that he may better relate and understand others. A one-dimensional personality is fragmented and cannot be trusted in a wholesome relationship that requires the totality of both parties. We need to see the depths of an individual, his physical and external being, as well as his spiritual, emotional, and internal make-up. We need to share all of this with our co-partners so that each can better cope with the adversities with which he/she is confronted, both inside and outside the home-place.

Authenticity
I'm proud to be of African descent.
My roots are rich; they're truly heavenly sent.

Authenticity is extremely important in assessing the true Africana family. It means that you are racially conscious and, therefore, true to your culture, as being culturally connected makes you not only love yourself and your heritage but protect and defend it as well. You will find yourself doing whatever it takes to improve the image of your race, which in not to be confused with inauthentic acts of assimilation. This is what too many Black people do, thinking that duplicating other's cultural values, such as those of the dominant culture, would make them better and more accepted and respected. Granted, there are some rewards that come with assimilation, but those rewards come as a sacrifice of one's self, indeed, a high price for surface gratification.

Flexible Role Player
I do what must be done at any given time,
In being the man, minus the crime.

In the Africana family, we must be flexible role players, for our duties and obligations are not cast in stone. We must shift or switch roles, according to the needs and demands of the family. The Africana man and woman are co-partners and, as such, they find themselves often having to cover each other's back, even to the extent of performing the traditionally assigned activities of the other. For example, if the man at some time finds himself jobless, the woman must assume the role of primary breadwinner without feeling that he is less a man because of it. In Terry McMillan's *Disappearing Acts*, which later became a movie, one of the two protagonists, the African man,

> Franklin necessarily has to take care of the house, which he does well … Franklin tries to accept their situation for the time being, but, of course, he has a difficult time not maintaining the traditional role of breadwinner.
> (90)

The chapter, "McMillan's *Disappearing Acts*: In It Together," continues the Africana Womanist analysis with equal attention given to the Africana man.

> *Respectful of Women*
> *I love and respect the woman, the center of life.*
> *She's deserving of this to help her avoid the strife.*

What does it take for the Africana man to realize that to disrespect his woman is to disrespect himself and his whole race? She is the mother of his children, the mother of the race and as such, deserves respect. Granted, the respect for her should be reciprocal, but it should naturally start here.

A very strong Africana womanist, Dr. Regina Jennings, does an excellent inside assessment, as a member of the Party, of the Africana man and women in the Black Panther Party during its early years. In her article in a Special Issue on Africana Womanism for *The Western Journal of Black Studies*, "Africana Womanism in the Black Panther Party: A Personal Story," she exposes the sexist behavior of one man in particular, the captain, whose acts represent disrespect for this female counterpart, which needed challenge:

> There were women in the Party like me who tried to hold on because we understood the power, the significance, and the need for our organization. Black men, who had been too long without some form of power, lacked the background to understand and rework their double standards toward the female cadre. Perhaps, if the Party had external observers—community elders who respected our platform—such unfair practices against women would not have occurred or could have been curbed. "However, all men in the Party were not sexist, and I must emphasize this, for as an Africana womanist, I am interested in both the truth and in my total race."
> (Jennings, *WJBS* 151)

Fortunately, this is not the position of most of the men in that organization, for not only must Africana men respect their women, they must also demand that others do so as well. Without the respect for the Africana woman, the Africana man and our race are not going very far.

Protector
It's nothing more than what's naturally expected—
Protecting our womenfolk from the evil projected.

The Africana man must always protect his woman. This mandate comes from God himself, as he assigns this duty to the man. He must stand by her side, ready to defend her in case of danger. This is not to suggest in any way that he must tower over her, dictating what she can or cannot do in terms of her choices or decision. It is only to assure her that her life is being guarded against any harm, hurt, or danger. In short, the Africana man must have his female counterpart's back.

Responsibility goes hand and hand with the role of the Africana man as protector. He must be accountable for both the financial and the emotional security of his children as a means of protecting them, too, from hurt and danger. The day of the single household, female mother-father, absentee father must be no more in the real sense. In other words, whether he is always physically there (the parents may have divorced or may have never married in the first place) should have very little or nothing to do with his responsibility to his children, as his presence in the sense of protecting and supporting them and their mother is very important for their future. Therefore, his involvement with his children in every sense is a requirement for the ultimate survival of our future generations. To move forward in a positive and progressive way, our children first need the survival of their family, at least in the sense of support, to which we must all aspire, including the fathers.

Moral
We honor all that's good, as God proclaims,
The purest heart and soul, will shape our aims.

Morality is another important feature for the Africana man. He must know that doing the right thing, doing what is good is a great attribute. In the case of deciding upon and holding to the commitment to family, this is critical, as too often today people fall into the snake pit of wallowing in the mud with people who are immoral, people who have no interest in or respect for the truly good things in life, which we must avoid at any cost.

Female-Compatible
We are the pair that creates the human race.
Without each other, humanity is not a case.

The cornerstone for the survival of the Africana family is male/female compatibility. Thus, for the Africana man, he must be female-compatible. He must love and honor his mate as the deserving precious jewel in his life. She would be the love of his life, as he should certainly be the love of her life. There is nothing more sacred and beautiful than a loving committed couple for the ultimate survival of the Africana family/community. Morrison's Sixo in *Beloved* comments on the beauty of such a relationship between the man and the woman:

> She ["Thirty-mile woman"] is a friend of my mind. She gather me, man. The pieces I am, she gather them and give them back to me in all the right order. It's good, you know, when you got a woman who is a friend of your mind.
>
> (Morrison 272–273)

Respectful of Elders
Our mothers and father we hold in high esteem.
It can't be otherwise; they set the dream.

Much like this quality for the Africana womanist, the Africana man, too, must demonstrate reverence and respect for his elders. They have been there for all of us from the beginning and having paid their dues for humankind, and particularly for our community, they are more than deserving of respect in their declining years on this earth. To disrespect them is to disrespect life itself.

Supportive
Unless I stand in support of all your needs,
We're left realizing only half our deeds.

Support of your co-partner is a large part of what it takes to make for a positive relationship. That support is physical, financially, emotional, and spiritual as well. Supporting each other on all levels, including also socially, and politically, in all the family affairs and decisions, is mandatory. This is not to suggest that you support your partner in unwise matters and choices, for it will surely be the demise rather than the fruition of a successful union with longevity.

Ambitious
Life holds so much for us to celebrate.
We must aspire to greater heights—Our fate!

Everyone needs someone to share the financial responsibilities of the household, be that in the capacity of both having jobs and careers or in the capacity of one staying home to care for the children, for example. Whatever the case, ambition is essential to helping to make ends meet for the security of the family. The Africana man must not fall prey to the jealousy monster and let go his own ambition due to the success of his mate. He must remain ever true to his own ambition to ensure that he has become all that he can in life.

Fathering and Loving
We must not separate our inclinations,
The basis for empathy is human sensations.

Finally, in successful parenting, the last two features of the true Africana man, fathering and loving, go hand in hand. You must not be afraid of taking control in circumstances when the opinions and rules of the father are critical to decision-making for the family. You must be firm in upholding the leadership role in the family, while at the same time show love and concern for your family, the mother, and the children, whose lives are indelibly impacted upon in virtually every way. Thus, the Africana man must demonstrate tough love when needed, thus enabling the child/children to grow up in a wholesome environment for a wholesome personal development. To be sure, loving and fathering are not to be feared; instead, these seminal qualities must always be revered. Hence, in conclusion,

> If all Africana men respected the original reality of the equality of both sexes in African cosmology, then they would refuse to continue to allow external forces, such as non-traditional African religions and alien political family structures wherein female subjugation is inherent, to influence their lives and ways. The end result would be that Africana people (men and women) the world over would then collectively struggle toward recovering their natural birth right as determiner of their fate as liberated people, dedicated to their families and their future generations.
> (Hudson (Weems), *Africana Womanism, 1st Edition* 144)

In short, Africana Womanism continues its insistence that there is no room for the Gender Divide, for, indeed, the gender divide can ultimately destroy our family structure. The Battle of the Sexes, then, would be of no consequence; therefore, this inappropriate separation of the genders would ultimately cease to exist! To be sure, it's men and women "In it together" for true humanity for all humankind!

Part II

Social Justice Long Overdue

Standing Strong

Summation List of 15 Positive/Negative Elements of Male-Female Relationships

Positive	*Negative*
1 Love	1 Contempt
2 Friendship	2 Rivalry
3 Trust	3 Distrust
4 Fidelity	4 Infidelity
5 Truth	5 Deception
6 Mutual Respect	6 Disrespect
7 Support	7 Neglect
8 Humility	8 Arrogance
9 Enjoyment	9 Mean-Spiritedness
10 Compassion	10 Callousness
11 Sharing/Caring	11 Selfish/Egotism
12 Complimentary	12 Negative Criticism
13 Security	13 Insecurity
14 Interdependence	14 Dependence
15 Spirituality	15 Non- Spirituality

(Reprint, Chapter VI, *Africana Womanist Literary Theory*, 2004, 79–97).

DOI: 10.4324/9781032720036-7

5 Debunking Excuses for Racism

Africana Legendaries A to Z

The best tactic for eradicating racism is to first debunk the racist excuses for its existence. For centuries, the dominant culture has tried to justify the low status of Africana people as being a result of biological inferiority, despite our massive contributions to society, refuting such a notion. This initiative was launched in 1926 as Negro History Week by Dr. Carter G. Woodson, the Father of Black Historiography, later becoming Black History Month in the 1960s. In 1980, as Founding Director of Black Studies at Delaware State U, I launched the highly respected tradition Outstanding Black Delawareans. Although many of us have transcended adversity to some degree, unimaginable racist practices continue to hold us back. Yet, as resounded in Maya Angelou's celebrated poem,

"Still I [we] Rise"
You may write me down in history
With your bitter, twisted lies,
You may tread me in the very dirt
But still, like dust, I'll rise.

Does my sassiness upset you?
Why are you beset with gloom?
'Cause I walk like I've got oil wells
Pumping in my living room.

Just like moons and like suns,
With the certainty of tides,
Just like hopes springing high,
Still I'll rise.

Did you want to see me broken?
Bowed head and lowered eyes?
Shoulders falling down like teardrops.
Weakened by my soulful cries.

DOI: 10.4324/9781032720036-8

Does my haughtiness offend you?
Don't you take it awful hard
'Cause I laugh like I've got gold mines
Diggin' in my own back yard.

You may shoot me with your words,
You may cut me with your eyes,
You may kill me with your hatefulness,
But still, like air, I'll rise.

Does my sexiness upset you?
Does it come as a surprise
That I dance like I've got diamonds
At the meeting of my thighs?

Out of the huts of history's shame
I rise
Up from a past that's rooted in pain
I rise
I'm a black ocean, leaping and wide,
Welling and swelling I bear in the tide.
Leaving behind nights of terror and fear
I rise
Into a daybreak that's wondrously clear
I rise
Bringing the gifts that my ancestors gave,
I am the dream and the hope of the slave.
I rise
I rise
I rise.
Indeed, with God in front, we will survive. And "To God Be the Glory."

Below are 26 Africana Legendaries, one representation for each alphabet from A to Z. There are 20 Africana Women and 6 Africana Men, which is a testimony to the fortuitous need to have a man represent those letters where a female representative was difficult to find. Thus, what is demonstrated here is that we must welcome, at all times. Our Interconnectedness—In It Together:

1—***Delores P. Aldridge, PhD*** (JUNE 8, 1941)—**Distinguished Grace T. Hamilton Founding Chair & Professor** Emerita of Sociology & Africana Studies, **Emory U**, Dr. Aldridge was the unprecedented **two-term President** of **NCBS** (National Council of Black Studies). With over 100 awards, including the Georgia Governors Award, this Educator/Activist **founded** the **first Africana Studies Program** in **Southern US**.

2—*Angela Bassett* (AUG 16, 1958)—**Actress**, **Producer**, **Director**, & **Activist**, Angela Bassett has starred in numerous films on the **real lives of Black women**. She has won numerous Awards, including the **Golden Globe Award** for *What's Love Got to Do with It*, **Black Movie Award** for *Akeelah & the Bee*, **NAACP Image Award** for Malcolm & the **Screen Actors Guild Award** for *Black Panther*.

3—*Alvin O. Chambliss, Jr., JD* (JAN 22, 1944)—"The **Last Original Civil Rights Attorney** in **America**," he was the Lead Counsel in the **Ayers vs Fordice** Supreme Court Case, winning **$500M** for HBCUs in MS in the battle against segregation of higher education. The 2006 Charles Hamilton Houston Distinguished Professor of Law at Indiana U, he, like Houston, "rather live[s] on [his] feet than to die on [his] knees."

4—*Angela Yvonne Davis, PhD* (JAN 26, 1944)—**Professor, Political Activist, Philosopher**, **Author, & Academician**, Dr. Angela Davis was once a member of the **Black Panther Party**. She, "In defense of Human Rights," is most known for her ongoing activities **fighting against the Industrial Prison Complex**.

5—*En Vogue* (1989–Present)—A **Top R & B pop vocal Black Female Group, En Vogue** became number two on the US Hot 100. The exceptionally talented group consists of four beautiful singers—Terry Ellis, Cindy Herron, Maxine Jones, and Dawn Robinson. Of their many hits, "Free Your Mind" remains popular even today.

6—*Aretha Louise Franklin* (MAR 25, 1942–AUG 16, 2018)—**Queen of Soul**, she was a recipient of many awards: received a star on the **Hollywood Walk of Fame** (1979); first female performer inducted in the **Rock & Roll Hall of Fame** (1987); the **Grammy** Lifetime Achievement Award (1994), & the **Presidential Medal of Freedom** (2005).

7—Pam Grier (MAY 26, 1949)—American **award-winning actress** and singer. Known as **cinema's first female action star**, she acquired fame early in her career, playing **iconic roles** in movies such as *Coffy* (1973) and *Foxy Brown* (1974). She continues her acting career, and played a major role in the ABC Sitcom, ***Bless This Mess*** (2019–20).

8—*Cathy Hughes* (APR 22, 1947)—**Entrepreneur**, **TV** & **radio personality, & business executive**, she is the **founder** of the media company **Radio/Urban One**. She became the **first African American woman to head a publicly traded corporation**. A minority owner of **BET** Industries, she launched **TV One** in 2004. She & **son, Alfred Liggins III,** were named Entrepreneur of the Year—Ernst & Young.

9—*Ice Cube*—(JUNE 15, 1969)—Ice Cube, **Rapper**, **Filmmaker**, **Actor,** & **Activist**, is an **award winner, honoree,** & **nominee**. A trailblazer, he puts much energy in the movie industry, focusing on **Black life** in our communities & controversial race issues, i.e., ***reparations*** for **native African Americans**, evoking **Dr. Obedike Kamau's** reparation call—**"*I Want My Money.*"**

10—*Mae Jemison, MD* (OCT 17, 1956)—**Engineer** and **Physician**, Dr. Jemison was the **first African American female astronaut** & the first African American woman **to travel into space**. A beautiful Black icon & a true model Black female pioneer.

11—*Dr. Alveda King, PhD* (JAN 22, 1951)—**Evangelist**, Civil Right **Activist Author**, she is the **Director of Civil Rights for the Unborn**. **Daughter of A.D. & Naomi King & niece of Dr. Martin Luther King Jr.**, she is a former State Rep. for the 28th District in the Georgia House of Representatives, & an official **commentator for *Fox News***.

12—*Henrietta Lacks* (AUG 1, 1920–OCT 1, 1951)—The **source of cells forming the HeLa line** comes from Henrietta Lacks, and it is used in controversial medical research since 1950, a year before her death. The case of **the use of her cells without payment or permission** from her or her family remains a question today.

13—*Toni Morrison* (FEB 18, 1931–AUG 5, 2019)—**Award-winning novelist** of about a dozen novels & several **non-fiction books,** such as **Playing in the Dark**, Morrison received the **National Book Critics Circle Award** for ***Song of Solomon***, the **Pulitzer Prize** for ***Beloved***, made into a **film**, etc. Moreover, in 1993, she became the **first African American female to win the *Nobel Prize for Literature*** for her body of work. In 2012, she received the **Presidential Medal of Freedom**.

14—*Diane Judith Nash* (MAY 15, 1938)—A **Civil Rights Activist** since her undergraduate years at Fisk U, she was a **1960s Freedom Ride organizer**, who risked her life numerous times, challenging America's violation of the human rights of African Americans in their quest for "Life, Liberty & the Pursuit of Happiness."

15—*Michelle Robinson Obama* (JAN 17, 1964)—**Attorney**, Author, & **Wife of President Barack Obama**, Michelle was the **first African American First Lady**. A Princeton University graduate, she, like her husband, finished **Harvard Law School** before embracing the political world. She is a model for many, initiating key concerns, i.e., health, relative to everyday life.

16—*Rosa Parks* (1913–2005)—**"The Mother of the Civil Rights Movement,"** Rosa Parks was a noted **Activist** who refused to relinquish her bus seat to a white man in **Montgomery, Alabama, on DEC 1, 1955**. Her demonstration evolved into **the 1956 year-long Montgomery Bus Boycott**.

17—*Quavo—Quavious Keyate Marshall* (APR 2, 1991)—**Rapper**, **Singer**, **Song Writer, & Music Producer**, **Quavo** is one of the three very talented **Migos** hip hop & trap rappers—**Quavo, Offset & Takeoff**. The group has won its second **Number One Album** in the US and numerous other awards. Inspiring!

18—*Kelly Rowland* (FEB 11, 1980)—African American **actress and singer/songwriter**. She was one of the **original** four R&B singers with **Destiny's**

Child, with Beyoncé. Her acting career has grown significantly since her lead role in The Seat Filler.

19—*Lillian A. Smith* (JAN 19, 1955)—For nearly two decades in the media industry, Lillian Smith served as former **Senior Producer** for the Emmy Award-winning worldwide syndicated TV talk show, ***Phil Donahue,*** & Executive Producer for **Fox TV in LA**. She fought to ensure **the inclusion of Black lives**—from entertainment, politics, academia, sports, womanhood, etc.—& t**he rights of Blacks to be televised worldwide** as a means of changing minds for the betterment of all.

20—*Cicely Tyson* (DEC 19, 1924–JAN 28, 2021)—Cicely Tyson is a highly **respected actress of over seven decades**. She is known for **her chosen roles of authentic African American women** as a part of a positive African American family. Former wife of the renowned musician Miles Davis (1981–1988), she was a recipient of numerous awards, including **four Black Reel Awards**, **three Emmy Awards**, a Tony Award, a **Peabody Award**, a Screen Actors Guild Award, and an **Honorary Academy Award**.

21—*Blair Underwood* (AUG 25, 1964)—**Actor**, **Director,** and **Producer**, Blair Underwood is a long-time stable Hollywood actor, who has played leading roles in both **Black and white films** & **television shows**. His latest act is a leading role in Netflix's "**Self-Made**: Inspired by the **Life of Madam CJ Walker**" (2020).

22—Dorothy Vaughan (SEPT 20, 1910–NOV 10, 2008); **Katherine Johnson** (AUG 26, 1918–FEB 24, 2020); **Mary Jackson** (APR 9, 1921–FEB 11, 2005)—Three iconic Black women mathematicians & engineers collectively played seminal roles in making possible the 1965 Apollo 11 spaceflight to the moon. **Vaughan**, a human computer, was NASA's first supervisor of the West Area Computers; Johnson, a master pioneer for the use of the computer, effected complex calculations for orbital mechanics; **Jackson**, an aerospace engineer, was NASA's first Black female engineer. All were award winners.

23—*Ida B. Wells-Barnette* (JULY 16, 1862–MAR 25, 1931)—**Anti-Lynching Crusader for Social Justice**, Ida B. Wells spent a lifetime fighting for the Human Rights of Africana people. As a **journalist**, she was brave in **exposing senseless, brutal lynchings** of African Americans in Memphis, TN, and the MS areas in particular. She received numerous death threats by whites should she ever return.

24—Malcolm X (Little)—El-Hajj Malik el- Shabazz (MAY 19, 1925–FEB 21, 1965)—An African American Muslin minister and leader, he was **a strong Human Rights Activist during the Civil Rights Movement**. He received the **Presidential Medal of Freedom posthumously**. He was assassinated on May 25, 1965.

25—*Josephine Silone Yates* (NOV 15, 1859–SEPT 3, 1912)—Yates was the **second Black Woman Full Professor at any US college or university**.

She was also the **first Black Woman Dept. Head**, Science—Chemistry, and English Literature and the **second President of the National Association of Colored Women**. A herald for Africana people, she was **a teacher-activist**, whose chief concerns remained with the family.

26—*Tukufu Zuber, PhD*—Antonio McDaniel (APR 26, 1959)—**Social Critic, Documentary Filmmaker, Professor, & Author**, Dr. Zuberi is one of the **hosts** of the long-running program **PBS *History Detectives***. He received the Best Director Award and the Best Documentary for his first film, ***Africa Independence***, for which he wrote the companion book, published by Rowman and Littlefield Publishers

These are just a few of the countless legendary Africana women (and men, too), who are showcased here because of the focus on the Africana womanist, representing us well in their myriad achievements. They have gone down in history and will continue to do so, as notable legendary Africana people. They are our models, not only for us, but for any living human being, whose aspirations and accomplishments are noteworthy. To be sure, they have demonstrated excellence in their many admirable talents, skills, brilliance, visions, etc., symbolizing their commitment to themselves, as well as to their loved ones, to never stop creating the much-needed victories and otherwise successes. AMAZING! The list continues and "To God Be the Glory."

The array of Legendary Africana Women, supported and protected by a select representation of our model Africana men, is to show that we have been and will always be "In It Together." Below is a select list of 15 important quotations by the author, relative to who we are as Africana women, which could be justifiably put on one's list of words of inspiration to be remembered:

Top 15 Quotations by the Author: Debunking Racism for Social Justice and Racial Healing

1 "While I am not calling for a replacement of traditional, established paradigms, I am nonetheless proposing a broadening of the body of criticism to include yet another perspective or paradigm, Africana Womanism, now evolving to Africana-Melanated Womanism." (***Africana Womanism: Reclaiming Ourselves*** 5th & 6th Editions 112 & 129)

2 "We are all members of the Human Race, and thus, are entitled to the same rights and privileges, demanding that policies/laws be put in place for just equity for all." (***Africana Paradigms, Practices and Literary Texts: Evoking Social Justice*** xv–xvi)

3 "Historically, Africana women have fought against sexual discrimination as well as race and class discrimination. They have challenged Africana male chauvinism but have stopped short of eliminating Africana men as allies in the struggle for liberation and familyhood." (***Africana Womanism: Reclaiming Ourselves*** 5th & 6th Editions 21 & 23)

4 "We need our own Africana theorists, not scholars who duplicate or use theories created by others in analyzing Africana texts." ("Africana Womanism and the Critical Need for Africana Theory" in ***Contemporary Africana Theory, Thought and Action: A Guide to Africana Studies*** 79)

5 "We as Africana people must decide for ourselves who we are and what our agenda need be [via] identifying our own demands, beginning with self-naming and self-definition." **("Self-Naming and Self-Definition: An Agenda for Survival,"** in ***Sisterhood, Feminisms and Power: From Africa to the Diaspora*** 451)

6 [Black Women] "stand resolute in upholding her duties and responsibilities to the children and our future generations. She must be Mothering and Nurturing, for molding character and caring for the physical and emotional needs of the children are critical for the continuation of a wholesome people/society." (***Africana Paradigms, Practices: Evoking Social Justice: Evoking Social Justice*** 5)

7 "The very foundation of the Africana-Melanated Womanism paradigm and movement is the primacy of the family and the collective struggle of our men and women together for the future of our children." (***Africana Womanism: Reclaiming Ourselves*** 5th & 6th Editions 119 & 136–137)

8 "Our ultimate success, including our social, economic, religious, and political persuasions, depends inevitably upon a collective Movement, one which unselfishly embraces the entire family—men, women and children." (***Africana Paradigms, Practices and Literary Texts: Evoking Social Justice*** 4)

9 "The fact remains that while the number one obstacle to success for Africana people is racism, the problem of sexism in our community continues to rear its ugly head, with the full knowledge that this problem is not only inauthentic but, more important, unfeasible since we are, after all, in a collective struggle for the survival of our entire family—men, women, and children." (***Africana Womanist Literary Theory*** 93)

10 "Africana people [are] in quest for our God-given birthright to true freedom for our families and communities." (***Africana Paradigms, Practices and Literary Texts: Evoking Social Justice*** xv)

11 "…Placing all women's history under White women's history, thereby giving the latter the definitive position is problematic. In fact, it demonstrates the ultimate of racist arrogance and domination suggesting that authentic activity of women resides with White women." (***Africana Womanism: Reclaiming Ourselves*** 5th & 6th Editions 13 & 15)

12 "What White feminists have done in reality was to take the lifestyle and techniques of Africana women activists and used them as models or blueprints for the framework of their theory, and then name, define and legitimize it as the only real substantive movement for women. Hence, when they define a feminist and feminist activity, they are, in fact, identifying with independent Africana women, women they both emulated and

envied." (***Africana Womanism: Reclaiming Ourselves*** 5th & 6th Editions 13 & 15–16)

13 "When Africana women come along and embrace feminism, appending it to their identity as Black feminists, or African feminists, they are in reality duplicating the duplicate." (***Africana Womanism: Reclaiming Ourselves*** 5th & 6th Editions 13–14 & 16)

14 "When the Black feminist buys the white terminology, she also buys its agenda." (***Africana Womanism: Reclaiming Ourselves*** 5th & 6th Editions 25–26 & 28)

15 "Dr. Martin Luther King, Jr.—the father of the Movement; Mrs. Rosa Parks—the mother of the Movement; **Emmett Louis Till—the child [and catalyst] of the Movement**, hence, a TRILOGY of a sort." (***Africana Womanism: Reclaiming Ourselves*** 5th & 6th Editions 123 & 141)

Along the same line in the last quotation on Dr. King, Rosa Parks, and the Movement, we have my nephew, **Matthew Harper** (1997–2022), a victim himself, who was very aware and always supportive of human vulnerabilities, i.e., the case resulting from racism, as symbolized in the 1955 infamous Emmett Till murder case.

6 Racism and Misogyny against the Black Family

From the Bible to the Street

I.

> As a race the most painful part of our experience with the Western world is the "dewomanization" of women of African descent. It is true that to successfully destroy a people its female component must be first destroyed. The female gender is the center of life, the magnet that holds the social cosmos intact and alive. Destroy her, and you destroy life itself.
>
> ('Zulu Sofola, *quoted in Foreword, Africana Womanism* xii)

The above quotation articulates well the painful and unjust verbal violation, let alone physical violation at times, that Black women suffer from both the Black man and the white man. For example, in the case of the latter, it is not so much the word "nappy" that we found offensive in the commentary of Don Imus, American radio personality and television talk show host, recording artist and author, in his widely televised, condescending ridicule of the Black basketball players at Rutgers University on April 4, 2007. He called them "Nappy Headed Hos," a racist statement that ignited nationwide response of rejection and disapproval, causing him his job, as many sponsors and companies pulled their advertisements and national Black leaders called from the cancellation of the television talk show, *Imus in the Morning*, which was granted. It was the context in which that word was used, the so-called assignment of who we, as Black women, are, although he noted that the foul expression, in fact, oddly originated in the Black community. For example, Black male rappers used the expression in their music. Be that as it may, the term "nappy" in and of itself is not negative. Quite the contrary, it is positive, authentic, and accurately descriptive, thus making it very much accepted in the Black community, and particularly among Black youths today. Our hair has been often described as "nappy" or "kinky" or "very curly" and positive; proud Black women, and men, too, for that matter, have not taken offense to its use as a consciously warm assessment of our hair. With Imus, on the other hand, we are called "nappy headed hos/whores" in a putdown, misogynistic fashion. The connotation is degrading, as it suggests that Black women are

DOI: 10.4324/9781032720036-9

promiscuous, "hos," and thus deserving of being used, abused, and called out of our names by any man, Black or white for that matter. Had we been called "Beautiful, nappy headed Black women," rather than "nappy headed hos," the whole controversy would never have happened.

There have been numerous books written by Blacks regarding the caring for natural Black hair, such as *Nappy Heads*. A number of children books, such as *Nappily Happy*, have also been written with positive connotations of the term and there are a growing number of Black beauty solons across the nation such as "Nappy by Nature" that promote and celebrate "nappy" hair as a symbol of beauty and authenticity for Black people. These natural hair salons, with every service imaginable for the caring of locks, comb coils/twists, braids, twist outs, and the long-standing afros, are astounding. To be sure, because of our pride in ourselves and our looks, we resent the insults of Imus and those of others, like our unconscious Black brothers who put down their own Black women. The inherent disdain and even ridicule that went with what Imus said on live TV, his syndicated talk show, *Imus in the Morning*, for all to hear, represent the ultimate act of disrespect of Black women which must now come to a halt.

It was in the Foreword to the first edition of *Africana Womanism: Reclaiming Ourselves* in 1993 that the late Dr. Zulu Sofola, Professor and Chair of the Department of the Performing Arts, University of Nigeria, Ilorin, made that profound commentary on the status of Africana women and the Africana family. It was a statement relative to Black women in particular and how the Western world has traditionally devalued her beauty and the sanctity of the Black woman and Black womanhood. This amazing icon, distinguished as Nigeria' first female playwright, was introduced to me following my presentation at the first International Conference for Women of Africa and the African Diaspora in 1992, which was held at the University of Nigeria–Nsukka. It was then that I invited her to write the Foreword to my manuscript, *Africana Womanism: Reclaiming Ourselves*, which she accepted. I had just recently completed it and was awaiting a global event to add the global touch to it. In that Foreword, Dr. Sofola's commentary was directed at the Western world's efforts to devalue the Black woman. However, it must be noted that many Black men have bought into the white man's perception of their women—their mothers, their sisters, their "loved ones" and their daughters—in that they, too, demonstrate disrespect and disregard for our being. Granted, the woman must hold herself up in high esteem, but admittedly it becomes difficult when her own men folk, her protector and her co-partner, have chosen to dishonor her very existence as well, thereby at times showing disdain for her physical and spiritual essence in many ways. Unquestionably a lot of work in the area of healing and reprogramming perceptions about the basic standard of beauty and the value system itself must be established, as many Black people have come to not love and appreciate themselves and their own, based upon the decisions they make and the positions they take relative to the dominant culture's attitude toward Black people.

The following are six raps/poems I wrote in 2007, in direct response to Don Imus' racist statement. In these poems, I addressed both Black men and women, relative to how we see and respect/disrespect ourselves and each other, and, moreover, how we respond to the way others attempt to define and name us without permission:

For Black Men

1. Love and Respect

Wonder why we imitate others' beauty?
It's 'cause you seek outside as your duty.
Wonder why we stoop so very hard to please?
It's 'cause you flee to others for your tease.

Today's male-female relationships,
History reveals, were shaped from outside.
Black men were taught to hate our sexy lips.
From whence comes power not to be denied.

History reveals we protected our men,
'Cause to protect us meant to risk their lives.
You were forced to shun our needs and not defend
Your mothers, daughters and your precious wives.

Conditioned not to love and respect us,
To see us other than beautiful queens.
You looked outside to make a royal fuss
Over outside mates as beauties for you kings.

2. It Ain't All Good

So only certain Black women are truly whores?
Others are working equals to you and yours.
Okay then there is something in the name,
But still it ain't all good with such a game.

Why can't we make those who are labeled dumb Become the opposite of who they have become?
Let's make them want to not be a chicken-head,
But respected beautiful Black sisters instead.

Now look at us with new-found self-esteem.
You thought we couldn't reverse the lower team.

Well, now you see how true beauty emerges
Since taking total control over all our urges.

3. Back It Up

Back it up—

The booty shaking,
The name calling,
The foul language and all.

The self-hatred,
The female bashing,
The male bashing and all.

The anti-love,
The anti-family,
The anti-God and all.

The time has come;
Your love will flip—
The bottom will top for some.

4. Gone

Own up to all your true prejudices!
In doing so, we must acknowledge our own.
The time is over now for hating on us;
The time for disrespect is truly gone.

Don't claim mistakes of modern hip hop
As the source of racist, malicious bogus words.
Don't even try to cover up your faults,
Which we must certainly now call to a halt.

5. No History, No Balance?

Give me back my history; give me back my life.
Without these things there is no real balance.
Don't take my history, please don't crush my life,
For God given knowledge will make the difference.

Did we just pop out to attack each other
Without true love for our sister and our brother?

Then blaming victims would justify your right,
Since there's no history, no basis to frame our sight.

6. Blessed Life

Life's for the living, so please let's live it now
Enjoy the real fresh fruits of blessed life—
Love, happiness, respect and a little bow
To Jesus Christ who granted us this life.

Up and away—the joys are for us all.
Let's kick it now into the right directions.
The woes must vanish 1st, lest we will fall.
Good times are positive ways to life connections.

Let's kick it all the way to true glory.
No need to avoid our much-deserved fun. Remember God does not believe in worry.
Now it's time for a powerfully loving bond.

We must now shift to cautioning Black Women to love both our Sisters and our Brothers. Stop destroying Sisterhood via hating on each other as a means of elevating selve. Moreover, stop thinking of Black men as our number one enemy, a position initiated by feminism as a concept designed to dismantle female subjugation.

7. Black Sisters, Stop! (2023)

In a nutshell, Sisters, please, **stop hating on each other**.
Trashing our sisters is not key to our love and success.
It's about continuing the bond between sister and brother,
In securing family love, security, and true happiness.

8. Our True Agenda (2023)

You know that **racism is our common enemy**,
As both Black men and women strive to transcend.
Racial domination is the very epitome
Of taking total control over all our kin.

Black. Women, just stop believing the hype—
That Black men seek to silence us as their foes.

The notion of **"breaking silence" is not our type**
Of things describing our real true-to-life goals.

This quest to move from **homeplace to workplace**
Is not a real issue for Africana women.
It's always been hard work we've had to face,
Since we'd been forced to work, just like our men.

As for our role of mothering and nurturing **our children**,
It's not to be construed as condescension,
Instead, we're serious about character molding,
For that's the surest way to enhance our mission.

9. I Love You (2023)

Black men throughout the many ages
Have shown true love for their significant others.
They've notated this reality on many pages
Of their recordings and those of other brothers.

"I love my lady, my woman, my babies' mom,
Who makes our needs her number one concern.
Her tasty, healthy meals are truly the bomb,
Created out of love, we've come to learn."

"I love my man, with all my heart, I do.
He's always there whenever I need him most.
Be it emotional or physical, he is my 'Boo.'
He's got me covered, and that's no empty boast.

II.

Africana Womanism Poetry Trilogy: From the Bible to the Streets

"Africana Womanism: Two-Sided Human Coin" (2023)

In the beginning God created the heaven and the earth.
...And God said, Let us make man in our image...
The male and female created he them.
God blessed them ... and *To God Be the Glory*

And so it was and so it is—the male & female together.
Family centrality—That's it. We're going nowhere without the other.
Collectivity, our true nature in all our acts,
Seeking love, and peace, and joy; and *to God Be the Glory.*

If we will recall the origins of Humankind—
All men are created equal, our Heavenly Father's design,
Life would be truly simpler; of course, you know by now;
Thus, victory for our entire family; and *To God Be the Glory.*

"Africana Womanism: I Got Your Back, Boo" (2009)

Don't you know by now, girl, we're all In It Together!
Family-Centrality—that's it; we're going nowhere/out the other.
That means the men, the women, and children, too,
Truly collectively working—"I got your back, Boo."

Racism means the violation of our constitutional rights,
Which creates on-going legal, and even physical fights.
This 1st priority for humankind is doing what it must do,
Echoing our 1st lady, Michelle—"I got your back, Boo."

Classism is the hoarding of financial privileges,
Privileges we must all have now in pursuit of happiness.
Without a piece of financial pie, we're doomed to have a coup;
Remember—protect the other—"I got your back, Boo."

Sexism, the final abominable sin of female subjugation,
A battle we must wage right now to restore our family relations.
All forms of sin inevitably fall under 1 of the 3 offenses:
A. W., "I Got Your Back, Boo," Corrects our common senses.

"Africana-Melanated Womanism: I Want My Boo Back" (2021)

They say my Boo, ain't worth an ounce of fuss.
Our choice is ours; it's totally up to us.
We choose our destiny; it's all in tack. Collectivity—"I want my Boo back!"

We're family, meaning all must stick together.
I need you; you need me; it's us forever.
No matter what, we're from the same authentic sack.
Connectivity—"I want my Boo back!"

Today it's anti-him; tomorrow it's me,
The sister others will not let her be.
Remember, jumping ships presents a serious lack.
Commitivity—"I want my Boo back!"

(Hudson (Weems), *Africana-Melanated Womanism*)

7 James Baldwin and Toni Morrison

Literary Crusaders for Social Justice

> As Toni Morrison said in her final tribute to Baldwin, his was "a life that refuses summation and invites contemplation instead … [with a] tenderness and vulnerability that asked everything of us, expected everything of us." ("Morrison's Quotation comes her assessment of Baldwin in *New York /Times* par. 3; Reed, The Essential James Baldwin: Life and Literature, At Home and Abroad," in *Africana Paradigms*)

In situating the common journeys of James Baldwin and Toni Morrison, two of our most revered activists, be they men or women, in their life-time dedication to the ultimate freedom of global Africana families in the quest for social justice, Dr. Pamela D. Reed, Professor and Founding Executive Director of the James Arthur Baldwin Africologic Institute (Virginia State U), cites Nobel laureate Toni Morrison, reflected in the above commentary, whose profound assessment of Baldwin interestingly reveals the commonality between the two. Much like Ida B. Wells, the historical anti-lynching crusader for social justice, they, too, are activists, more specifically, Literary Crusaders for Social Justice. They commit their lives to justice for all Blacks, indeed, the case for countless other notable historical activists, who boldly and bravely fought for our birth rights as human beings. Baldwin contends that

> What began here is a history of identity, not only inaccessible, but also systematically and deliberately denied and destroyed.
>
> (Baldwin, *"On Racism"—The Dick Cavett Show*, 5/16/1969)

The above quotation is Baldwin's commentary on the history of Black American identity, which he offered on "The Dick Cavett Show" in 1969, during which time he debated Yale University Philosophy Professor Dr. Paul Weiss. Eighteen years later in a 1986 National Press Club Speech, nine months prior to his unfortunate demise in 1987, Baldwin continues this focus on the massive impact of racism on the African American family. During that speech in Washington, DC, he asserts the following, relative to the most important

DOI: 10.4324/9781032720036-10

issue on the future of America— racism and its relativity to human freedom and American Democracy:

> I think we are going to have to re-think everything we think is true now because it's not going to be true tomorrow … to accommodate ourselves … is to re-think and re-create our vocabulary, which includes the human race. We are all, in this room, at the mercy of, whether or not we know it, European vision of the world, and that vision is obsolete.
>
> (*CSPAN, December 10, 1986, Washington, DC*)

Twelve years later, in 1998, Baldwin's kindred spirit, Nobel laureate Toni Morrison made a similar assessment of the destiny of America, relative to the significance of racism. She continues the idea of re-thinking race relations in terms of re-creating the language, layered with deep meanings, both connotative and denotative. This is needed in properly defining the real foundation of a workable solution to end racial dominance, wherein Morrison makes a clear distinction between race and racism:

> There is no such thing as Race. It's just a Human Race—scientifically, anthropologically. Racism is a construct, a Social Construct, and it has benefits. Money can be made off it. People who don't like themselves feel better because of it. It can describe certain kinds of behavior that are wrong or misleading. So, it has a social function—Racism. But race can only be defined as a Human Being … And when you take it [the "ism"] away ("I take your race away."), then there you are, all strung out and all you got is your little self. And what is that? What are you without your racism? Are you any good? Are you still strong? You still smart? You still like yourself? If you can only be tall because somebody's on their (sic) knees, then you have a serious problem. And my feeling is that white people have a very serious, serious problem. And *they* should start thinking about what *they* can do about it. Take me out of it.
>
> (Morrison, *Interview with Charlie Rose*)

The quotation is a serious commentary by the author in an interview for *The Guardian* with Charlie Rose. During their lengthy conversation, Morrison speaks of an interesting interview she had the year before, 1997, with a white European female journalist who asked her if she had ever imagined writing a novel not centered on race, Black people, to which Morrison sternly replied,

> You can't understand how powerfully racist that question is, can you? as you could never ask a white author, "When you going to write about Black people?" whether he did or not, she did or not. Even the inquiry comes from a position of being used to being in the center and saying, "Is it ever possible that you would enter the mainstream?" It's inconceivable

> that where I already am is the mainstream … I stood at the border, stood at the edge, and claimed it as central, and let the world move over to where I was.
>
> (Morrison, *Interview* 1997)

Morrison, then, asked the journalist if she had ever asked a white writer if he or she had ever thought about writing about Black people, rather than about themselves, white people. The point here is that the dominant culture thinks that it is fine to write about white people, placing themselves at the center of any and everybody's narrative, thereby implying that if Black writers truly expect to be successful, then, they, too, must write about white people, which commands that they, too, place whites at the center of their story and/or analysis. Of course, Morrison totally disagrees with this notion, insisting that their assumption—that to be successful, white people must hold the center position—is unquestionably a racist posture. She refuses to succumb.

In June 1985, my co-author, Dr. Wilfred Samuels of the U of Utah, and I, Founding Director of Black Studies at Delaware State University, spent an intimate full day, interviewing Morrison in her New York home on the Hudson River, just prior to my first semester as a doctoral student at the U of Iowa in African American Studies. During the interview, she vowed to continue to write about her chosen subject, Black people, whose lives are richly layered with a multitude of experiences and ideas, far richer than others care to imagine, thus never ceasing to tell our stories and passing them on:

> I am really happy when I read something, particularly about black people, when it is not so simple minded … when it is not set up in some sociological equation where all the villains do this and all the whites are heroes, because it just makes black people boring; and they are not. I have never met yet a boring black person. All you have to do is scratch the surface and you will see. And that is because of the way they look at life.
>
> (Samuels and Hudson (Weems), *Toni Morrison* 1)

To be sure, Black life is life, in its totality, imbued with boundless activities, emotions, and memories, that can never be reduced or relegated to the status of non-existence.

Much like Ida B. Wells-Barnett, the Anti-lynching Crusaders for Social Justice, except that they are "Literary" Crusaders for Social Justice, these powerful two position their characters to play out the roles of activists. Remaining true and committed to Africana people, the two are, indeed, the personifications of the flip sides of the Human Coin, epitomizing the long-existing battle against brutal racism. Moreover, they represent life-long activities as model philosophical international icons, "the drive behind the very nature of the interconnectedness of the Africana man and woman, given the inseparable bond" (Hudson (Weems), "Africana-Womanism: Authenticity and Collectiveness" 15). We must be ever cognizant of the dominant and obtrusive nemesis, the race factor, which surrounds virtually every aspect of Black life, thereby necessitating the race factor as the number one priority for saving our lives. Both are serious, resolute writer-activist, *artivists*, who passionately embraced their responsibility of participating in establishing ownership over their individual lives and the lives of the broader Africana community, insisting upon fighting for true freedom on all fronts via their protest literary works. Morrison proclaims that "the function of freedom is to free somebody else," which is, indeed, a political act (Morrison's Cinderella Stepsister's Commencement Address, Bernard College, 1979). Baldwin, too, is resolute, proudly proclaiming, "I am not your Negro" in the spirit of "thinking black" and working together, collectively pulling us out of the racist depths of degradation, disrespect, and relegation.

But the heated debates by both Baldwin and Morrison started earlier with the former, back in 1965, the year of major landmarks, including the signing of the Voting Rights Act, following the 1964 Civil Rights Act signed by President Lyndon B. Johnson. That was the 1965 James Baldwin vs William Buckley Legendary Debate—"Has the American Dream Been Achieved at the Expense of the American Negro?" at the Cambridge Union, Cambridge University England. Baldwin victoriously defended his position on the matter of racism, white privilege, and the economy, wherein he insisted that the dilemma of the African American can no longer be dismissed or ignored, as the great American Dream has been predicated upon the exploitation of Blacks. He won the debate, with 544 votes in agreement with his position, whereas Buckley, on the other hand, received only 164 votes, thus making Baldwin's point that blatant exploitation of African Americans is every bit worth the heated debate then, and even now, as the nuances of the controversial debate yet reign high:

> Now, we're speaking about expense … The economy, especially of the Southern States, could not conceivably be what it has become if they had not had and do not still have, indeed, and for so long, so many generations, cheap labor. I am stating very seriously, and this is not an over-statement: "I picked the cotton & I built the railroads … for nothing, nothing … created by my labor and my sweat and the violation of my women and the murder of my children". This, "in the land of the free and the home of the brave", and no one can challenge that statement. It's a matter of historical record.
>
> (Baldwin vs Buckley, 1965)

Now comes the question of the validity for Reparations, which Dr. Raymond A. Winbush describes in his book, *Should America Pay? Slavery and the Razing Debate on Reparations*, as

> …compensation plans for crimes against humanity … It is a Movement that continues to "make sense" to those who wish to understand the

so-called "Black-White Wealth Gap," crime rates in African communities, "educational gaps," and "health disparities" in those same communities. Once reparations are achieved for the global Africana community, it will liberate them economically, psychologically, and spiritually, but will also begin the long and arduous process of liberating the descendants of Europeans from a false sense of superiority over their accomplishments, long thought to be of their "ingenuity" rather than their violence.

(*Winbush Networks of Steel: Reparations* 139 &145)

This is a serious commentary, as reparations, a sort of atonement, really make sense as we reflect on Baldwin's reminder of the fact that the hard labor alone, without compensation for African Americans for centuries, came to an absolute naught for us, economically speaking. Only whites benefited via "white privilege." Malcolm X's Reparations Speech in Paris, France—delivered on Nov 23, 1964, a year before his tragic death on Feb 21, 1965—makes an excellent case of the legitimacy of reparations:

If you are the son of a man who had a wealthy estate and you inherit your father's estate, you have to pay off the debts that your father incurred before he died. The only reason that the present generation of white Americans are in a position of economic strength … is because their fathers worked our fathers for over 400 years with no pay … We were sold from plantation to plantation like you sell a horse, or a cow, or a chicken, or a bushel of wheat … All that money … is what gives the present generation of American whites the ability to walk around the earth with their chest out … like they have some kind of economic ingenuity. Your father isn't here to pay. My father isn't here to collect. But I'm here to collect and you're here to pay.

(Malcolm X, 1964, *Paris, France*)

In this speech, he makes it clear that so-called "white supremacy" is, in reality, a myth, for the real basis for white "economic ingenuity" is racism and the exploitation of Blacks, thereby yielding whites' economic wealth. Baldwin continues,

And another way, this "Dream" is at the expense of the American Negro: … Until that moment comes when we, the American people, are able to accept the fact … that on that continent we are trying to forge a new identity for which we need each other. And that I am not a ward of America. I am not an object of missionary charity. I am one of the people who built the country. Until this moment, there is scarcely any hope for the American Dream because the people who are denied participation in it, by their very presence, will reck it. And if that happens, it's a very grave moment for the West.

(Baldwin vs Buckley 1965)

Racism, a social construct that renders racists great benefits, indeed, is designed and orchestrated by the dominant culture, the primary culprit, and, hence, we must continue to challenge it in our quest to overthrow it. This can be better achieved if we stick together in dismantling that design to bring our life goals to full fruition—a collective Victory for us as well. The gains and security, invariably regarded as inter-generational wealth, then, must be achieved by Black, too, and then passed on to our children and our future generations. This is not to be construed as being at the expense of others. Instead, it is to rightfully include us as recipients, thus enabling our life's mission to reach fulfillment as well as others. Hence, all will enjoy the American Dream, inevitably bringing forth true Social Justice for all.

Understanding the centuries of abject servitude Blacks have suffered in the US for nearly five centuries (beginning with the landing of the very first Slave Ship in 1526, nearly a century before the landing of the official first Slave Ship in 1619), Baldwin, like Morrison, knew too well how deep and serious our dilemma was and continues to be even today. According to Dr. Jacqueline Roebuck Sakho,

> Social and legal events unfolding around racial and economic equity, place the potentiality of an interest convergence opportunity on the horizon. The sociopolitical and sociocultural atmosphere in 2020 demonstrates what might be discussed as a convergence of legal, educational, and policy interests.
>
> (Sakho 46)

The relativity of unresolved issues, creating continuous toxicity and total deprivation on all fronts, attests to the fact that the ongoing system of racism is, indeed, even more intolerable today, evidenced in the continuous heated and swelling national/international debates and demonstrations as we speak. The national demonstrations in response to the murder of 46-year-old George Floyd in Minneapolis, Minnesota, pleading for his life—"I can't breathe," were followed by international demonstrations, after the televised footage of that murder, begging the officer to take his foot off his neck. But he was not the only victim during this time, as countless others died during that fateful year of the early stages of the 2020 raging Coronavirus:

> The following is a small sample of Black victims ["Emmett Till Continuums"] during the first half of 2020: Ahmaud Arbery, 25; Breonna Taylor, 26; George Floyd, 46 and Rayshard Brooks, 27, three of whom were slain by officers whose primary mission is to protect as guardians, not kill as warriors.
>
> (Hudson (Weems), *"The Civil Rights Movement"*
> *The Columbia Daily Tribune* 2)

Of course, this phenomenon goes back countless centuries for Africana people and must now be called to a halt. In this respect, Baldwin and Morrison, in their literary, historical works, remained resolute to their end. They demonstrated absolute commitment, centering their efforts on totally eradicating racism by destroying its roots, grounded in greed, massive misinformation about who Blacks are and what they have contributed to society, as well as their terrible senseless need to dominate.

In 1964, Baldwin's definitive Civil Rights play, *Blues for Mr. Charlie*, inspired by the 1955 brutal lynching of 14-year-old Emmett Louis "Bobo" Till of Chicago, was published. In my 1988 pioneering Ford doctoral dissertation, "Emmett Louis Till: The Impetus of the Modern Civil Rights Movement," published in 1994 as *Emmett Till: The Sacrificial Lamb of the Civil Rights Movement*, I dedicated a whole chapter, "Artistic Responses," to identifying key literary authors who highlighted Emmett in their responses to the Civil Rights Movement of the 50s and the 60s: Arthenia Bates' short story, "Lost Note," Gwendolyn Brooks' poem, "The Last Quatrain of the Ballad of Emmett Till," Anne Moody's autobiography, *The Coming of Age in Mississippi*, and Endesha Ida Mae Holland's play, *From the Mississippi Delta*, and James Baldwin's *Blues for Mr. Charlie*. The following is my commentary on Baldwin's play:

> The fact that the dominant culture would frequently, without reservation, inflict the cruelest forms of violence on an oppressed people, as in the case of the Till lynching, clearly establishes the fact that blacks are the most despised group and are more victimized by such heinous crime, as tools of social control ... The intent of the dominant culture is to control the African American and hold him or her in a subordinate position.
>
> (Hudson (Weems), *Emmett Till* 124)

However, we must hold America accountable for such a mindset, for we, as Baldwin asserts in his "Notes for Blues,"

> ...have the duty to try to understand this wretched man [the murderer]; and while we probably cannot hope to liberate him, begin working toward the liberation of his children.
>
> (Baldwin, *"Notes for Blues"* 6)

This, indeed, takes responsibility to a new level.

Baldwin's *If Beale Street Could Talk* (1974) is also an excellent example of the artist/activist. The novel ends on a note of ambiguity, given the future of the two protagonists—Tish and the love of her life, Fonny, whose unjustifiable incarceration was made possible by a racist white police officer who enforced the false accusation of rape by a Puerto Rican woman. Predicated upon the cruel and abrupt separation of the devoted couple, who became unable to raise their child together, the fate of their new-born, too, was up in the air, his birth, signaling a new fragile generation, as he "cries and cries and cries and cries and cries and cries and cries and cries and cries like it means to wake up the dead" (Baldwin).

Artivist Morrison, too, went to the bottom of the issue to find meaning beneath the surface in her novels, wherein her characters play out the author's primary messages. For example, in her Pulitzer Prize-winning novel, *Beloved* (1987), her narrator made the following assessment, relative to the plight of the Black woman:

> That anybody white could take your whole self for anything that came to mind. Not just work, kill, or maim you, but dirty you. Dirty you so bad you couldn't like yourself anymore.
>
> (Morrison, *Beloved* 251)

Indeed, she gets to the core of the matter and delves into the psychology/psychosis behind the white man's acts, relative to taking ownership of the Black woman's body and mind. He takes total control of her total being, to the point of dictating how she feels about even herself, her lack of respect for her being, and, by extension, in many cases, how she feels and relates to her family.

Baldwin and Morrison, both deep thinkers and activists, are respected for their inclinations to scratch beneath the surface for true meaning and understanding, particularly as we contemplate the American dilemma, which cannot be separated from the African American dilemma. In their own ways, their efforts suggest that they concur with the fact that we are all "In It Together"—men, women, and children in a concerted effort to bring Victory to our people, "free at last" from the vicious throes of racial dominance. It is this collectivity, which pre-Africana Womanist activist and author of *A Voice from the South* (1892), Anna Julia Cooper, insists upon: "Woman's cause is man's cause. We rise or sink together, dwarfed or Godlike, bound or free," thereby compelling us to remain a collective in the war against racism on all fronts (Cooper 61).

The opening stanza of the signature poem, "Africana Womanism: I Got Your Back, Boo," succinctly captures the essence and power of the Africana Womanism family-centered paradigm, calling for collectivity for our success:

> Don't you know by now, girl, we're all In It Together!
> Family-Centrality—that's it; we're going nowhere without the other.
> That means the men, the women, and children, too,
> Truly collectively working—"I got your back, Boo."
>
> (Hudson (Weems), *Africana Womanism* 120 & 137)

Clearly, James Baldwin, representing the male side of the Human Coin, and Toni Morrison, the flip side of the coin, the Africana womanism, are, in fact, mirror images of each other in both ideology and practice/action. They demonstrate a natural authentic propensity to embrace and execute the top priority for Africana people—debunking racism—wherever we are, be it in Europe, Africa, America, or elsewhere. We are the supreme paradigm of the wonders of being on the same page — "…having the same love, being of one accord of one mind" (*Philippians* 2:2)—as well we should for ultimate victory for all. These two highly respected icons left a powerful legacy of intellectual and political excellence for us to emulate, as they were not only accomplished authors in their own rights, but they were also passionate activists as well. We must own what is ours now—our God-given right to "Life, Liberty and the Pursuit of Happiness."

Enough of the lies, the misconceptions, "the true ugliness of American racism staring us in the eye!" as in the case of the bloated face of Emmett Till (Hudson (Weems), *Emmett Till*). We must now demonstrate real savvy, *Sankofa*, by reviewing our past and learning the endless lessons to avoid repeating the mistakes. We can, then, swiftly move forward, at last enjoying our long-deserved gifts of life, as promised by God. With this mindset, we are able to better realize our possibilities. The collective legacy of Baldwin and Morrison, their vast contributions as salient Literary Crusaders for Social Justice, represents both Collectivity and Connectivity on the part of Africana men and women, ideologically together for the ultimate victory for all Africana people. "To God Be the Glory."

8 Conclusion

> *Africana Womanism* is today's clarion call for Black People to wake up, "Stay Woke," and recognize that by whatever name we call Black women—Mama, Grandmother, Grandma, Madea, aunt, auntie, sister, daughter, niece, cousin, granddaughter, mother-in-law, sister-in-law, girlfriend, sistah, baby, honey, sweetheart, dear, my boo—they are our Mitochondrial DNA, the givers, nurturers and sustainers of Black Life and Culture.
>
> (Charles Williams, PhD, Professor Emeritus & Chair of Africana Studies, U of Memphis; former Dir of *Ida B. Wells-Barnett Institute for Social Justice*, Rust College)

The above statement, made by a colleague and friend, Dr. Charles Williams, who (with his wife, Dr. Hilda Williams, Professor, U of Memphis, retired, and former professor at Rust College) co-authored the insightful chapter on the Anti-Lynching Crusader for Social Justice—"Pre-Africana Womanist, Ida B. Wells-Barnett: Embodiment of Africana Womanism Principles." This was the opening chapter for Part III, "Moral Responsibility & General Wealth: An Africana Womanism Perspective," of my edited volume, *Africana-Melanated Womanism: In It Together* (2022). Indeed, what better way to define Africana Womanism than with the perfect model of the true Africana Womanist—mothering and nurturing in caring for the children by identifying and respecting her traditional, defined, and divine roles within the family structure. This is who we are, Ida B. Wells-Barnett, lavishing love and affection on her entire family. She is soft and loving, and tenderly attends to family needs. I am here reminded of a wonderful reception, celebrating the premier publication of *Africana Womanism: Reclaiming Ourselves* in the fall of 1993, during which time, one of my astute and supportive colleagues, Dr. Bob Bender, Professor of English and Women and Gender Studies at the University of Missouri, shared his attitude toward and thoughts on the theory of Africana Womanism. In a newspaper coverage of the event, he, who happens to be white, expressed his belief in and support of the theory, pointing out the Power of Self-Naming and Self-Defining for people in general, and, in this case, for

DOI: 10.4324/9781032720036-11

Black Women, as this is a major cornerstone as the first 2 of 18 characteristics of the theory itself:

> Naming is important and one of the problems with being named by some other group is that you are not who you want to be. Until you have the right to give a name to yourself and to what you are doing, you have no power whatsoever. Africana womanism is a fine idea.
>
> (Bender, *Mizzou Weekly* 7)

A few years later, I was invited to Temple University—the home of the first Africana Studies Department to offer a PhD in the field—where I delivered a paper on the importance of Africana Womanism in preparation for challenges of the new millennium:

> As we approach the last hour leading up to the next millennium, I cannot stress enough the critical need today for Africana scholars [and people] throughout the world to create our own paradigms and theoretical frameworks for assessing our works [and acts]. We need our own Africana theorists, not scholars who duplicate or use theories created by others....
>
> (Hudson (Weems), *"Africana Womanism and the Critical Need"* 97)

Those were my exact words 2½ decades ago, 1997, in "Africana Womanism and the Critical Need for Africana Theory and Thought." Enough of the misnaming ("neither an outgrowth nor an addendum to feminism") of the Africana Womanist after someone else, whose model may have very well been the Africana woman (*Africana Womanism* 15). That was the very reason I set out in the first place to name, define, and refine a paradigm for us, all Africana women and our wonderful families as well. From that, at last comes the creation of this short manuscript, designed for a broader community, both inside and outside academia, while serving as an overview, as well as a guide for making possible a better life for each of us in our daily pursuits of joy, justice, and true victory. To be sure, our world is in desperate need of truth, love, and passion to affect a healing, for racial wrongs, indeed, have yet to be corrected or satisfied adequately.

Now that we have a fuller picture of the presence and the divine role of the Africana Womanist within the context of her family, it must be made clear that the inherent message in *Africana Womanism: An Introduction to Elevate Humanity* for the dominant culture is to respect the original law outlined in the *Declaration of Independence*—"We hold these truths to be self-evident, that all men [and women] are created equal, that they are endowed, by their Creator, with certain unalienable Rights, that among these are Life, Liberty, and the pursuit of Happiness" (July 4, 1776). With that in mind, it goes without saying that whites, too, have the responsibility of doing what is right, fair, and just. In short, they must join in the commitment to rectify historical wrongs by ensuring true justice for all humanity, understanding that until all is free, none is free in a real sense. Admittedly, this is more than an issue for Africana people. It's a human issue for all, and thus, like the Africana womanist, all must protect and regard the destiny of the human family, including Blacks, by unselfishly and collectively embracing a strong sense of true family centrality. The sense of priorities, the needs of all (the human family), as opposed to the needs of the individual (the woman exclusively), informs the theory of Africana Womanism, highlighted as a means by which the humanity of all can be elevated in our quest for ultimate salvation—no matter the gender, no matter the ethnicity. Now is past time for us to swiftly move forward. And "To God Be the Glory."

SELF-EVALUATION: Thoughts, Suggestions, and Considerations

1 What is Africana/Africana Womanism & its priorities?
2 What features of Africana Womanism do you see in yourself?
3 What are some of those elements seen in others, i.e., family or friends?
4 What features would you be most interested in for improving your personality?
5 How can Africana Womanism heal the anti-male sentiments that Betty Friedan calls for an end to in her 1981 sequel, *The Second Stage*, earlier suggested in her 1963 Women's Lib book, *The Feminine Mystique*?
6 Did Toni Morrison's 1971 *New York Times* article, "What the Black Woman Thinks about Women's Lib" (a critique of Betty Friedan's *The Feminine Mystique*: "Too much emphasis is placed on gender politics") influence the author?
7 How can Africana Womanism's family centrality close the race and gender divide for all that is wreaking havoc on our society and our families?
8 What are some of its positive effects on the children?
9 List additional positive features not listed among the existing 18 characteristics.
10 Why are your additional characteristics significant?
11 Is Africana Womanism workable for other ethnicities, as we are all members of one race, with a multitude of ethnicities?
12 What are some of the Africana Womanism features evidenced in some Africana Legendaries?
13 Make a list of other Legendary Africana People, both men and women, who could be identified as Africana Womanism or its supporters.
14 Why is Africana Womanism a special though "yet another theoretical concept?"
15 How could Africana Womanism positively impact society, whether or not one chooses it as a model for oneself?
16 List benefits of sharing Africana Womanism, both inside and outside academia?

References

Bender, Bob. Quoted in the *Mizzou Weekly* in response to the September 1993 release of the new book, *Africana Womanism: Reclaiming Ourselves*, Dr. Bob Bender was quoted in support of the theory of "Africana Womanism."

Hudson (Weems), Clenora. "Africana Womanism and the Critical Need for Africana Theory and Thought." *The Western Journal of Black Studies* 21, no. 2 (Summer 1997), 79–84.

CODA

Representing the voice of the new millennium are two of my former graduating students. The first one is Black and the other is White, both presenting in their oral Power-Point reports the applicability of Africana Womanism theory in varied fields of study, specifically here in Authentic Social Work by utilizing Africana Womanism features as a tool of analysis, and ending with the "Adultification" of Black Children, black girls in particular, by imposing adult mannerism on them during their earlier stages of growth and development. In utilizing the various characteristics of the paradigm, we can achieve major life goals for our families and, by extension, for all humankind, as we are all members of one race—The Human Race. Thus, from these two reports, we have a glimpse of bringing forth true Social Justice for all humanity:

1 Africana-Melanated Womanism: Tools of Analysis for Social Work by Alexis Seals
2 A Practical Application of Africana-Melanated Womanism to Society for Young Black Girls: Ending "Adultification" of Black Childhood by Samantha Keel

I. Africana-Melanated Womanism: A Social Work Tool of Analysis -- (AS)

"In It Together"—A Program for Black Women: Africana Womanism Characteristics and Their Connection with the Field of Social Work.

Africana Womanism characteristics can be used across all fields. Below is the connection between Africana Womanism and the field of Social Work:

Social Work Values

- Service
- Dignity and worth of a person
- Social justice

DOI: 10.4324/9781032720036-12

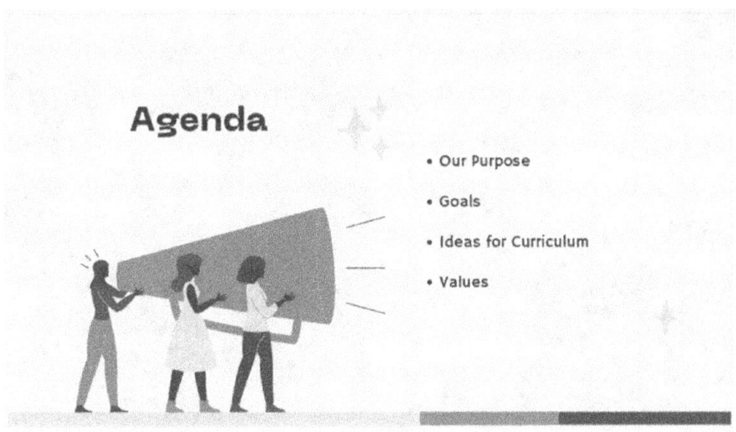

Figure 9.1 Overall Agenda for Africana Women.

Figure 9.2 Key Purpose for Sisterhood.

Africana Womanism Addresses the Need for the Liberation for All Humankind

- Competence
- Integrity
- Importance of Positive Human Relationships

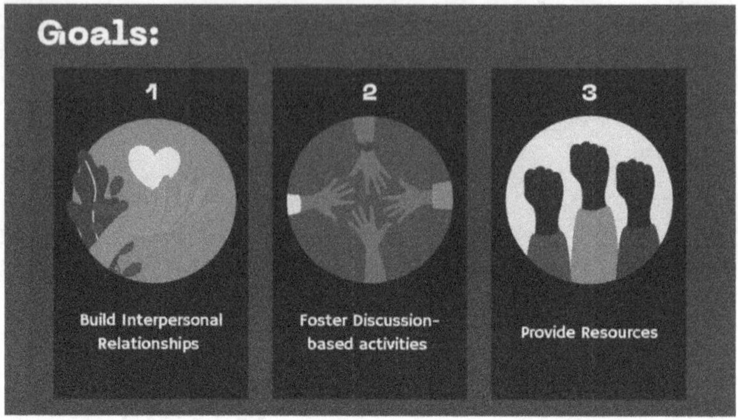

Figure 9.3 Goals for the Family.

What Is the Purpose of This Program?

To create a space for Black women to come together, form a natural sisterhood for healing and growth in their own community.

Africana Womanism Values for Program

Strong (Physical, Emotional, & Spiritual)
Nurturing
Mothering
Genuine in Sisterhood
Respect
Authentic
Family centeredness

On the matter of **Genuine Sisterhood**, the program can build strong relationships to foster growth and development.

Why Does Africana Womanist Theory Help to Guide Programs?

In addressing the particular needs of all, and in this case, Africana women, it makes possible workable resolutions for yet another member of another ethnicity, too long and too often marginalized. Hence, specialization commands tools for addressing concerns in supporting true cultural diversity.

Why Is It Preferred over Feminism or Black Feminism?

The program has a focus of **family centrality**, a historical practicing mandate, as one of the main building blocks.

Goals

To Build interpersonal relationships .....
To Foster discussion-based activities .....
To Provide resources .....

References

Clenora Hudson (Weems). *Africana Womanism: Reclaiming Ourselves*, Fifth Edition. London and New York: Routledge, 2020.

II. A Practical Application of Africana-Melanated Womanism to Society for Young Black Girls: Ending "Adultification" of Black Childhood—Samantha Keel

I had a best friend when I was around 12 or 13 years old. We had the same first name, liked the same shows, hobbies, clothes, music, etc., and shared at least one class every school year until she moved away in the eighth grade. Something that I remember being different between us, however, is just how differently adults treated us. She was the one who would get called out in class for talking, even though I was the one who started the conversation. She was also spoken to differently as it wasn't how they talked to me. I remember that she dressed differently, too, not the brands, because I remember us gushing about the clothes we saw at Justice. It was their fit. I don't have a single memory of her wearing anything other than long, slightly baggy pants and U-neck T-shirts. She also talked differently, but not in a dialectical way. I always thought she was so cool because she spoke in a way that adults did. She sometimes swore in school and wasn't afraid to get sassy with the kids who bullied me because we were the best of friends.

As an adult, I now know why we were treated so differently. I was white, and she was black. We were both too young at the time to realize how wrong and unfair this was to her. The term for what the adults in our lives were doing to her, "adultification," wasn't formally a term until 2008, nor was its use widespread until 2017. "Adultification" is defined as "a form of racial prejudice where children of minority groups, typically Black children, are treated by adults as being more mature than they actually are." It acts as predatory conditioning that leaves our children vulnerable to mistreatment, harassment, abuse, and even death in the worst-case scenarios. While there haven't been many formal studies or investigations into the effects of adultification in American society, there have been two major studies. One in 2014, headed by Phillip Atiba Goff and Matthew Christian Jackson of the University of California, "Los Angeles, on the Effects of Adultification of Black Boys," and "Girlhood Interrupted: The Erasure of Black Girls' Childhood" by Rebecca Epstein, Jamilia J. Blake, and Thalia Gonzalez of Georgetown Law Center on Poverty and Inequality in 2017.

"Girlhood Interrupted" is especially invaluable, as it covers subjects that have been often dismissed or ignored by scientists, academics, and activists for at least decades. These issues are problems like sexualization and victim blaming, medical mistreatment and neglect, and domestic abuse in multiple forms. But all is not lost. If we, as a community, as parents, family, friends, etc., take the time to address the problem, we could change thinking into something that can lift our young Black girls instead of oppressing them, despite racist acts of others. The purpose of this essay is to argue that if we take the problem of "Adultification" and look at it through the framework of Africana-Melanated Womanism, then we will have raised a generation of Black women who value and appreciate themselves and are willing to teach other and new generations Africana Womanist ideas, thus helping to break the cycle of oppression. To do this, I will examine each problem the study brings up. I will analyze it through the framework of an Africana-Melanated Womanianist scholar, Dr. Clenora Hudson (Weems), to offer solutions to each aforementioned problem.

One of the first problems addressed is that Black girls are thought to need less nurturing and less protection. Researchers asked 325 adults, primarily white and female, at 74% and 62%, respectively, and 69% of all respondents held a degree beyond a high school diploma, to complete a questionnaire about their perceptions of white or black girls. The questionnaire results found that respondents believed Black girls were more adult than white girls, particularly in areas such as the level of nurturing and protection they need. However, the most significant part of this experiment is that as early as five years of age, black girls were more likely to be viewed as behaving and seeming older than their age in nearly every stage of their life (Epstein et al., p. 8). Because of this belief that black girls are more mentally mature than their white peers, black girls have different expectations placed on them and are given far more severe punishments than their white peers. With this knowledge, Epstein and her team theorized that if authorities in public systems view Black girls as less innocent, less needing of protection, and generally more like adults, it appears likely that they would also view Black girls as more culpable for their actions and, on that basis, punish them more harshly, despite their status as children (Epstein et al., p. 8).

What will help fix this issue is if we make our communities more family-centered, which is the cornerstone of one of Hudson (Weems)'s 18 features of Africana-Melanated Womanism. We should emphasize to these girls that they are loved as daughters, granddaughters, nieces, cousins, friends, etc., and not as "young women" or whatever term adults will use. This is not to disrespect them, especially those who may be older, such as the study's 10–14- and 15–19-year age range, but, instead, so that they understand that they are allowed to act like kids. It is not their job to shoulder the load of a guardian or caretaker when they already must worry about education, extracurriculars, friends, and, God forbid, puberty for the older girls! To summarize, let the structure of the family function as it is supposed to. When a parent or guardian takes the time to remove whatever emotional, social, or physical load they have given their daughters, they are helping in her emotional and physical growth, as well as bringing themselves up as more responsible caretakers.

Next is the fact that people think black girls need less support. Professor Edward W. Morris recorded multiple teachers making extremely disheartening comments about Black girls. They were recorded, saying things such as "[T]hey think they are adults, too, and they try to act like they should have control sometimes," "describing Black girls as exhibiting" "very 'mature' behavior socially (but not academically), 'sophisticated,' and 'controlling at a young age'" (Epstein et al., p. 5). Professor Morgan even says, "Such comments demonstrate that stereotypes of Black girls, interpreted as 'loud', are imbued with adult-like aspirations, and perceived, in turn, as a threat" (Epstein et al., p. 5). It's heartbreaking to imagine that a grown adult would perceive a child as a threat to their station, baffling even that someone who is supposed to be a nurturing and supportive figure to a child, number two only to her parents, would trash call a kid in such a way. As a former education major myself, this was especially heartbreaking to read.

So how can we combat this problem? The answer lies in the very girls these teachers talk about coldly. A child's school years are integral to social development, and many variables can positively and negatively affect that growth. A family-centered home is such a positive development force that it significantly bolsters familial ties, provides a foundation for social growth, and boosts educational learning. These good foundations offer a space for black girls to become confident in themselves and become self-namers and self-definers, which are two more critical features of Africana-Melanated Womanism. Allowing Black girls to name and define themselves will break them out of the boxes of stereotypes that adults will try to cram them into, hence spreading that liberation to other girls. As quoted in the study:

> "Caricatures of Black femininity" are often deposited into distinct chambers of our public consciousness, narrowly defining Black female identity and movement according to the stereotypes described by Pauli Murray as "female dominance" on the one hand and loose morals on the other hand, both growing out of the roles forced upon them during the slavery experience and its aftermath (Epstein et al., 2017, p. 5).

So, what will happen when we have many courageous, strong, self-confident girls, running around refusing to be called "loudmouths" and "disruptive"? Most likely, several lunch detentions and arguments with disrespectful adults. But the communities built from a family-centered ideal will not let that stand. Plenty of examples around the US prove just how much a supportive community can change people's ways of thinking and that they can influence policy change that not only silences unsupportive and disrespectful authority figures but can change policies to be more supportive of demographics, such as Black girls.

Finally, the most disheartening thing is that Black girls are more independent and know or assume to know more about adult topics and sex. The stereotype of the hypersexual Jezebel feels far more widespread than it used to be, given how pop culture has changed into being far more encouraging of sexual liberation. While the concept of sexual liberation in and of itself is far from an evil idea, it is evil that adults will mutate the concept of being confident and knowledgeable about your body into something simultaneously shameful and fetishy. Professor Jamilia Blake and her colleagues of this study found that these stereotypes underlie the implicit bias that shapes many [adult's] views of Black females as sexually promiscuous, hedonistic, and in need of socialization. Teachers may subconsciously use stereotypical images of Black females to interpret Black girls' behaviors and respond more harshly to Black girls who display behaviors that do not align with traditional standards of femininity in which girls are expected to be docile, diffident, and selfless (Epstein et al., 2017, p. 5). This is especially essential to understand, because Blake uses the word diffident. Defined as "modest or shy because of a lack of self-confidence," there is not a more perfect word in the English language to define what precisely terrible adults want out of Black girls. One of the most dangerous consequences of "adultification" is the abuse of children. The solution to this problem is a bit more straightforward, yet probably the most difficult to execute of any other solution due to it requiring a lot more fighting concepts than power structures. The problem is that we let predatory adults create systems of shame that oppress our Black girls and change them into something manipulatable. Furthermore, "adultification" also causes Black children to be perceived as biologically older. The study cites a case where a police officer arrested a 15-year-old Black girl for using a student MetroCard because the officer perceived her as being 19 years old. He even refused to believe either of her parents when they also affirmed that she was within the legal age to use the card over the phone and held her in cuffs until her mother came and presented him with the child's birth certificate (Epstein et al., 2017, p. 6). The solution is that we need to let little Black girls be authentic little girls. Let these children act like children. Let them be silly, outrageous, messy, angry, playful, selfish, accident-prone, etc., in the same way that I, as a little white girl, was allowed to be. Little Black girls should be able to be authentic little girls without the shame and fear that predatory adults will try to enforce on them through issues like victim-blaming, body-shaming, misinformation, and intimidation.

Issues such as "adultification" are very disheartening to read and learn about. Activism has been, is, and always will be an emotionally, mentally, and physically draining calling. However, if we, as a population, encourage the research, study, and analysis of ourselves to serve better the next generation, such research would save vast amounts of pain and labor. We could use the data and conclusions from these studies to improve parenting, teaching, child welfare, and much more. If we raise our girls to be strong, loving, and whole, they will pass on that love and knowledge to their children, thereby making the fight for equality easier for everyone because we are all in this fight together. That's the Africana-Melanated Womanism commitment to the Africana family!

References

Epstein, R., Blake, J., & Gonzalez, T. "Girlhood Interrupted: The Erasure of Black Girls' Childhood." *Georgetown Law*, 2017. https://genderjusticeandopportunity.georgetown.edu/wpcontent/uploads/2020/06/girlhood-interrupted.pdf

Hudson (Weems), Clenora. *Africana-Melanated Womanism: In It Together*. England: Cambridge Scholars Publishers, 2022.

Hudson (Weems), Clenora. *Africana Womanism: Reclaiming Ourselves*. London and New York: Routledge Press, 2020.

Epilogue

Laura Faith Kebede-Kwumasi, BA/MA—Distinguished Journalist in Residence, Institute for Public Service Reporting, U of Memphis, Coordinator of Civil Wrongs

> Africana people are advancing to a higher plateau, the relativity of an important all-inclusive paradigm considering racial global issues on all fronts … actively engaging in the urgent struggle for human survival against the odds of race, class and gender oppression, the cornerstone of the prioritization for Africana Womanism.
>
> (Hudson (Weems), *Foreword in Rediscoursing African Womanhood: Africana Womanism* xiii)

For decades, Dr. Clenora Hudson (Weems) has been at the forefront of making space for Black women to name and define themselves, while also opening the door for others to benefit from these principles as well. Yet, take one look around our world today, and you'll see many seeking to be unlinked with any responsibility to anyone else. Considering the centuries of oppression toward women, the response is understandable. But it's short-sighted, for in a world that elevates "me" over all else, it's high time (again) to emphasize "we" in everything we do. Individualism has little place in the collective struggle for freedom. Given this fact, while Black women must be unapologetic about the unique perspectives we bring to the world, we cannot afford to exclude Black men in our efforts. As Hudson (Weems) insists, "We need each other." Indeed, this is the foundation upon which the theory and praxis of Africana Womanism rests!

As a journalist, I see Africana Womanism's priorities of race, class, and gender most reflected in Ida B. Wells-Barnett's life and work. Her bold writing and investigative prowess were first realized in her concern for her race. She knew that the issues that Black women faced uniquely from Black men could not be addressed without demanding that society first see the humanity in her race. Hence, Dr. Hudson (Weems)'s Africana Womanism and the

DOI: 10.4324/9781032720036-13

prioritization of race first, then class, followed by gender clearly validates why she calls early iconic revolutionary icons, like Ida B. Wells, as well as Harriet Tubman and Sojourner Truth pre-Africana Womanists, instead of pre-feminists. In fact, in her latest edited volume, *Africana-Malanated Womanism: In It Together* (2022), Chapter 8, "Pre-Africana Womanist, Ida B. Wells-Barnett: Embodiment of Africana Womanism Principles," which was written by Drs. Charles and Hilda Williams, accurately names and defines Ida B. Wells-Barnett.

Her primary work, especially in her early years, was reporting on the rampant lynchings and the rise of Jim Crow, particularly in the South. In a natural and expected manner, since Black men and women invariably share racial oppression, she partnered with many Black men in this work along the way, including the man who became her husband, Ferdinand Barnett, and the father of her four children. Like the Africana womanist, the needs of her family were just as important as her advocacy and society-changing work. In Chicago, she turned toward creating systems to help Black migrants from the South gain as much economic independence as they could because of how race and class were (and still are) interwoven in America. It was only then that she turned her gaze toward the Women's Suffrage Movement, later called the feminist Movement, which she believed was liberal during its beginnings, as they at least ostensibly shared the quest for equal voting rights. However, Wells soon found massive resistance from white women, who had become hostile and racist toward Black women, resulting from the 1870 ratification of the 15th Amendment to the Constitution, which granted Black men the right to vote, while excluding women. The suffragettes disallowed room for Black women in their struggle, and thus Wells ended her association with this antagonist force against Black life including the Black woman.

For too long, many white Americans have not seen their destinies as tied to Africana people. It's evident in feminist theory, class struggles, and, of course, in our nation's enduring racist patterns. So, the responsibility fell upon Black people to chart a path to freedom for ourselves that recognizes the fact that we are all interdependent, interconnected, and can only flourish when we are all free. Victory in this sense would look like children's character and curiosities being nurtured in a loving environment, elders being cared for and remembered, men being content rather than in competition for their place in the world, and women being encouraged to attend to their needs as they do everyone else's. This is what we strive for in Africana Womanism, a collective movement for men and women together in protecting our children and ensuring a legacy for our future generations. And we need it more than ever today. Clenora Hudson (Weems)'s 2009 Africana Womanism signature poem, **"Africana Womanism: I Got Your Back, Boo,"** articulates this well in its opening stanza, wherein lies the key to our ultimate survival—knowing, understanding, and appreciating our truth, as ordained by God—powerfully issued forth, hence mandating total victory:

> Don't you know by now, girl, we're all In It Together!
> Family-Centrality—that's it; we're going nowhere /out the other. That means the men, the women, and children, too,
> Truly collectively working—"I got your back, Boo."
>
> (Clenora Hudson, *"Africana Womanism: 'I Got Your Back, Boo'"* 2009)

Afterword

A.J. Stovall, PhD, Dean, Division of Social Behavior Sciences; Professor of Political Science; Founder, African American Student Leadership Conference (1993–2012), Rust College

> In the beginning God created the heaven and the earth … And God said, Let us make man in our image, after our likeness; and let them have dominion over the fish of the sea, and over the fowl of the air, and over the cattle, and over all the earth, and over every creeping thing that creepeth upon the earth. So God created man in his own image, in the image of God created he him; male and female created he them. And God blessed them, and God said unto them, Be fruitful, and multiply, and replenish the earth, and subdue it.
>
> (Genesis 1: 1 & 26–28)

Implied in the opening Bible verse above is that the man and the woman were created by God as a unit, designed to work together in acquiring the mission assigned by God to "subdue," meaning to overcome, which appropriately evokes one of the cornerstones of the theory of Africana Womanism—"In it together." In reviewing Dr. Clenora Hudson (Weems)'s transformative work, *Africana Womanism: An Introduction to Elevate Humanity*, I am compelled to look closely at the nature of God's creation of the man and the woman by also reflecting on the significance of naming and defining Africana women and men and the concept of the Africana family. In this Epilogue, I explore how the book illuminates the true essence of Africana women and their counterparts in the transformative power of a profound love for and trust in the Creator, as well as in each other.

In the Foreword to Dr. Hudson (Weems)'s edited volume, *Africana Paradigms, Practices and Literary Texts: Evoking Social Justice*, Judge Joe Brown opens with the following assessment of the plight of the Africana man and woman at the expense of the Africana family:

> Protecting womanhood and promoting manhood: These things humans have been about forever as they are inherent in the process of breeding and

DOI: 10.4324/9781032720036-14

> providing for the next generations of the species. At the root of this human cycle is man and woman, working together to build and maintain families. These fundamental concerns and aspects of humanity are presently at risk in a world in which extended families are gradually fading away with each passing year. This is particularly true in the Africana community….
>
> The National problems are many; preeminent is the long-standing contradictions and inequities of the racial dynamic it has with its formerly enslaved citizenry. The traditional normative worldview sums itself with this observation: The human house will soon fall if it is divided. Men and women need each—if only to secure procreation and the proper rearing of offsprings. Masculinity is not only descriptive of conditions and nature, but proscriptive of internal control.
>
> (Brown ix)

Throughout the pages of this book, Hudson (Weems) invites us into a profound journey of self-discovery and empowerment, emphasizing the importance of African people reclaiming their identities from the oppressive narratives that have historically sought to diminish their worth. As a liberating force, she discusses the notion of an "authentic family-centered" concept for all women of African descent, first acknowledging the Africana family as a vital unit in the liberation and elevation of Africana people. Hudson (Weems) emphasizes the interdependence and interconnectedness of Africana men and women, recognizing their shared struggles and the need for unity. By fostering love, trust, and cooperation within the Africana family, this book underscores the potential for collective transformation and liberation.

Central to this transformative journey is the profound love for and trust in the Creator and each other. Hudson (Weems) highlights the spirituality that anchors Africana women and men, emphasizing the significance of faith and spiritual connectedness in their quest for liberation. Through a deep sense of love and trust, Africana people can draw strength, resilience, and guidance, fostering a collective consciousness that propels them toward a more liberated and equitable future. In defining the Africana woman, Hudson (Weems) recognizes her as a multidimensional being, deeply rooted in her cultural heritage, and shaped by the interconnectivity of various identities. She acknowledges the Africana woman's strength, resilience, and unwavering determination in the face of adversity. By celebrating her unique experiences and perspectives, the book affirms the Africana woman's agency, challenging the erasure and marginalization she has long endured.

The book clearly calls for Africana people to embrace their shared humanity, recognizing that their liberation is intrinsically tied to one another. By cultivating love, trust, and solidarity, the collective Africana people can dismantle the systems of oppression and create a world where their full humanity is recognized and celebrated. As acknowledged by Dr. Jacqueline Roebuck Sakho, my kindred advocate for the training of Leadership for African American

Students, in her chapter in *Africana Paradigms, Practices and Literary Texts: Evoking Social Justice*,

> In the practice of Africana Womanism's tenet of self-naming [and self-defining], I am a Black woman, mother, adult educationist. I occupy this space as resistance and liberation for myself, for the Black man as my counterbalance, for my children and thus, by extension, the Black community.
>
> (Sakho 43)

Through this profound connection with each other, as ordained by the Creator, Africana people can embark on a revolutionary journey toward liberation, self-definition, and self-determination.

In conclusion, let us carry forward the wisdom imparted by Clenora Hudson (Weems). Let us embrace the power of naming and defining Africana women and men, recognizing their worth and agency. Let us foster deep love, trust, and interconnectedness within the Africana Family, understanding that their collective liberation is intertwined. Finally, let us cultivate a profound love and trust in the Creator and each other, knowing that through this transformative power, Africana people will rise, elevate, and reclaim their rightful place in the world.

Bibliography

Aldridge, Delores P. "Confronting Plagiarism: Busted." In *The Definitive Emmett Till: Passion and Battle of a Woman for Truth and Intellectual Justice*, ed. Clenora Hudson (Weems). Bloomington, IN: AuthorHouse, 2006, 151–152.

Angelou, Maya. "Still I Rise." In *Still I Rise: A Book of Poems*. New York: Random House, 1978.

Aptheker, Bettina. "Strong Is What We Make Each Other: Unlearning Racism within Women's Studies." *Women's Studies Quarterly*, 9, no. 4 (Winter, 1981), 13–16.

Asante, Molefi Kete. "Afterword." In *Africana Womanist Literary Theory*, ed. Clenora Hudson (Weems). Trenton, NJ: Africa World Press, 2004, 137–139.

Bâ, Mariama. *So Long a Letter*. Great Britain: Heinemman, 1989.

Baldwin, James. *Blues for Mr. Charlie*. New York: Dell Publishing, 1964.

Baldwin, James. *If Beale Street Could Talk*. New York City: Dial Press, 1974.

Baldwin, James. "On Racism--The Dick Cavett Show"—Interview with James Baldwin and Paul Weiss, 1969.

Baldwin, James. "James Baldwin vs William Buckley: Has the American Dream Been Achieved at the Expense of the American Negro." National Educational Television (NET), 1965.

Baldwin, James. "National Press Club Speech." In Washington, DC: DEC 10, 1986.

Bender, Bob. "Africana Womanism and the Power of Self-Naming." In *Mizzou Weekly*, SEPT 1993.

Blassingame, John W. *The Slave Community: Plantation Life in the Antebellum South*. New York: Oxford University Press, 1979.

Christian, Barbara. *Black Feminist Criticism: Perspectives on Black Women Writers*. New York: Pergamon, 1985.

Christian, Mark. "Afterword." In *Africana Womanism: Reclaiming Ourselves*, 5th & Sixth Edition by Clenora Hudson (Weems). London & New York: Routledge, 2020, 131–133 & 2023, 151–153.

Coles, Steward, and Pasek, Josh. "Intersectional Invisibility Revisited: How Group Prototypes Lead to the Erasure and Exclusion of Black Women." In *Translational Issues in Psychological Science* 6, no. 4, (2000) 314–324.

Cooper, Anna Julia. *A Voice from the South*. New York: Oxford University Press, 1988.

Crooks, Robert, and Karla, Baur. *Our Sexuality*. Redwood City, CA: Benjamin-Cumming, 1990.

Davidson, Nicholas. *The Failure of Feminism*. Amherst, NY: Prometheus Books, 1988.

Evans, Sara. *Personal Politics: The Roots of Women's Liberation in the Civil Rights Movement and the New Left*. New York: Knopf, 1979.

Franklin, Clyde W. II. "Black Male-Black Female Conflict: Individually Caused and Culturally Nurtured." In *The Black Family: Essays and Studies*, ed. Robert Staples. Belmont: Wadsworth, 1986, 106–113.

Gordon, Vivian. *Black Women, Feminism, and Black Liberation: Which Way?* Chicago: Third World Press, 1987.

Haas, Jeffrey. *The Assassination of Fred Hampton: How the FBI and the Chicago Police Murdered a Black Panther*, Revised Edition. New York: Lawrence Hill Books, 2020.

Hare, Julia. "Feminism in Black and White." Quoted in *Black Issues in Higher Education*, by Mary- Christine Phillip. 11, March 1993, 12–17.

Harrison, Algea. "Attitudes Toward Procreation among Black Adults." In *Black Families*, ed. Harriette Pipes McAdoo. Beverly Hills, UK: Sage, 1981, 199–08.

Hill, Patricia Liggins, general editor. *Call and Response: The Riverside Anthology of the African American Literary Tradition*. Boston: Houghton Mifflin, 1997.

Hudson (Weems), Clenora, Editor. *Africana Paradigms, Practices and Literary Texts: Evoking Social Justice*. Dubuque, IA: Kendall Hunt Publishing, 2021.

Hudson (Weems), Clenora. "Africana Womanism and the Critical Need for Africana Theory and Thought." In *The Western Journal of Black Studies* 21, no. 2 (1997), 79–84.

Hudson (Weems), Clenora. "Africana Womanism: Authenticity and Collectiveness in Securing Social Justice." In *Africana Paradigms, Practices and Literary Texts: Evoking Social Justice*, ed. Clenora Hudson (Weems). Dubuque, IA: Kendall Hunt Publishing Company, 2021, 3–22.

Hudson (Weems), Clenora. "Africana Womanism." In *Sisterhood, Feminisms & Power: From Africa to the Diaspora*, ed. Obioma Nneameka. Trenton, NJ: Africa World Press, 1998, 149–162.

Hudson (Weems), Clenora. *Africana Womanism: Reclaiming Ourselves* Fifth & Sixth Editions. London and New York: Routledge, 2020/2023 respectively.

Hudson (Weems), Clenora. *Africana Womanism; Reclaiming Ourselves* First Edition. Troy, MI: Bedford Publishers, 1993.

Hudson (Weems), Clenora. *Africana Womanist Literary Theory*. Trenton, NJ: Africa World Press, 2004.

Hudson (Weems), Clenora, Editor. *Africana-Melanated Womanism: In It Together*. UK: Cambridge Scholars Publishing, 2022.

Hudson (Weems), Clenora. "Civil Rights Then and Now: Anti-Racism to Stop Emmett Till Continuum in a 5 Step Solution." In The *Columbia Daily Tribune*, June 20, 2020.

Hudson (Weems), Clenora. "Cultural and Agenda Conflicts in Academia: Critical Issues for Africana Women's Studies." *The Western Journal of Black Studies* 13, no. 4 (1989), 185–189.

Hudson (Weems), Clenora. *Emmett Till: The Sacrificial Lamb of the Civil Rights Movement*. Troy, MI: Bedford Publishers, 1994.

Hudson (Weems), Clenora. "Foreword." In *Rediscoursing African Womanhood in the Search for Sustainable Resistance: Africana Womanism in Multi-Disciplinary Approaches*, ed. Itia Muwati et al. Harare: College Press, 2012, xii–xv.

Hudson (Weems), Clenora. "Self-Naming and Self-Definition: An Agenda for Survival." In *Sisterhood, Feminisms and Power: From Africa to the Diaspora*, ed. Obioma Nneameka. Trenton, NJ: Africa World Press, 1998, 449–452.

Hudson (Weems), Clenora. *The Definitive Emmett Till: Passion and Battle of a Woman for Truth and Intellectual Justice*. Bloomington, IN: AuthorHouse, 2006.

Jackson, Deborah. "Foreword." In *Africana-Melanated Womanism: In It Together*, ed. Clenora Hudson (Weems). UK: Cambridge Scholars Publishing, 2022, x–xiv.

Jennings, Regina. "Africana Womanism in the Black Panther Party: A Personal Story." In *The Western Journal of Black Studies* 25, no. 3 (Fall 2001), 146–152.

Ladner, Joyce. "Blurb." In *Africana Womanism: Reclaiming Ourselves*, ed. Clenora Hudson (Weems). Troy, MI: Bedford Publishers, 1993.

Ladner, Joyce. *Tomorrow's Tomorrow: The Black Woman*. Garden City: Anchor, 1972.

Madondo, Gracious. "Why Africa Relates to Africana Womanism." In *The Southern Times: The Newspaper for Southern Africa*, July 19, 2018.

Malcolm, X. *Reparation Speech*. Founding Rally of the Organization of Afro American Unity (OAAU), Paris, France, 1964.

McMillan, Terry. *Disappearing Acts*. New York: Viking, 1989.

McMillan, Terry. "Hers." In *The New York Times*, October 15, 1987.

Moniuszko, Sara, and Bacchus, Danya. "Black Americans Experienced 1.6 million Excess Deaths Compared to White Population Over 22-year Period, Study Finds." *CBS News*, New York, 2023.

Morrison, Toni. *Beloved*. New York: Alfred A. Knopf, 1987.

Morrison, Toni. "What the Black Woman Thinks About Women's Lib." *New York Times Magazine*, August 1971.

National Center of Educational Statistics. "Degrees Conferred by Race/Ethnicity and Sex." 2023.

Ntiri, Daphne. "Introduction." In *Africana Womanism: Reclaiming Ourselves* Fifth & Sixth. ed. Clenora Hudson (Weems). London and New York: Routledge, 2020 & 2023, 1–8 & 1–9.

Ntiri, Daphne. "The WAAD Conference & Beyond: A Look at Africana Womanism." In *Sisterhood, Feminisms and Power: From Africa to the Diaspora*, ed. Obioma Nnaemeka. Trenton: Africa World Press, 1998, 461–463.

Reed, Pamela D. "The Essential James Baldwin: Life & Literature, Home and Abroad." In *Africana Paradigms, Practices and Literary Texts: Evoking Social Justice*, ed. Clenora Hudson (Weems). Dubuque, IA: Kendall Hunt Publishing Company, 2021, 53–68.

Sakho, Jacqueline Roebuck. "Black Women Adult Educators — *The Utterers of Black Leadership Preparation: An Africana Womanism and the Afrocentric Praxis*." In *Paradigms, Practices and Literary Text*, ed. Clenora Hudson (Weems). Dubuque, IA: Kendall Hunt Publishing Company, 2021, 33–50.

Samuels, Wilfred D., and Clenora, Hudson (Weems). *Toni Morrison*. Boston: Twayne, 1990.

Sofola, 'Zulu. "Feminism and the Psyche of African Womanhood," presented at Conference on Women of Africa and African Diaspora, University of Nigeria-Nsukka, July 1992.

Sofola, 'Zulu. "Foreword." In *Africana Womanism: Reclaiming Ourselves* Fifth and Sixth Editions, ed. Clenora Hudson (Weems). London and New York: Routledge, 2020 & 2023, xi–xii.

Steady, F. C. ed. *The Black Woman Cross-Culturally*. VT: Schenkman Books, 1981.

Taylor, Tammy S. "From Public/Private Schools to the Academy: Africana Womanism — Interconnectivity and the Africana Family." In *Africana-Melanated Womanism: In It Together*, ed. Clenora Hudson (Weems). UK: Cambridge Scholars, 150–162.

Truth, Sojourner. "And Ain't I a Woman." In *Narratives of Sojourner Truth*. New York: Arno and *New York Times*, 1968.

Wheeler, Barbara. "Africana Womanism: An African Legacy: It Ain't Easy Being a Queen." In *Contemporary Africana Theory, Thought and Action: A Guide to African Studies*, ed. Clenora Hudson (Weems). Trenton, NJ: Africa World Press, 2007, 319–331.

Winbush, Raymond A. "Networks of Steel: How Reparations for European Enslavement of Africans Unite the African Diaspora." In *Paradigms, Practices and Literary Texts: Evoking Social Justice*, ed. Clenora Hudson (Weems). Dubuque, IA: Kendall Hunt Publishing Company, 2021, 33–50.

Appendix
Africana Womanism Syllabus

Africana Womanist Writers of the 20th & 21st Centuries

Africana Womanist Writers—20th and 21st Centuries
Tuesday/Thursday (11:00 to 12:15)
Instructor: Dr. Clenora Hudson (Weems), Professor of English
Websites

hudsonweemsc@missouri.edu
https://english.missouri.edu/people/hudson-weems
https://en.wikipedia.org/wiki/Africana_womanism
https://en.wikipedia.org/wiki/Clenora_Hudson-Weems

Course Description, Rationale, Goals, and Objectives Only

Africana Womanist 20th & 21st Writers is an Undergraduate (4420) and Graduate (7420) Level Course designed to broaden one's scope from a family-centered perspective relative to issues, recurring themes, trends in modern Africana women fiction, highlighting its applicability to our everyday lives worldwide. A study of the lives and selected works by four leading Africana women writers—Global Prize-winning author Mariama Bâ (*So Long a Letter*), Nobel laureate Toni Morrison (*Beloved*), popular culture novelist Terry McMillan (*Disappearing Acts*), and award-Winning novelist Angie Thomas (*The Hate U Give*)—will be enhanced by careful readings of four theory books—*Africana Womanism: Reclaiming Ourselves,* 6th Edition, *Africana Womanist Literary Theory*, and *Africana-Melanated Womanism: In It Together*—as well as readings of scholarly selections by and about the various authors and their books. We will highlight the prioritization of Race, Class, and Gender, a major cornerstone of this paradigm, committed to empowerment and equality of all.

For Part I, students will be introduced to an authentic Africana theoretical concept, Africana Womanism, and for Part II, they will be applying it to the four Africana womanist novels. Together, all materials will enhance students' understanding of critical current issues relevant to Africana women and their families/communities.

The ultimate objective of the course, then, is to enhance one's knowledge and appreciation of Africana women and their interconnection with their families (men and children) in particular and Africana life and culture (historically and currently) in general. Its purpose is to introduce students to a relatable theoretical construct, as a possible antidote to some of the other female-based theories, such as feminisms. An authentic Africana paradigm designed specifically for all women of African descent, and, by extension, for all men and women in general, the paradigm demonstrates that we are, after all, IN IT TOGETHER!

Course Description, Rationale, Goals, and Objectives

Africana Womanist 20th and 21st Century Writers is an Undergraduate (4420) and Graduate (7000) Level Course, specifically designed to broaden one's scope from a family-centered perspective in the area of issues, recurring themes, and/or trends in modern Africana women fiction, highlighting its applicability to our everyday lives worldwide. A study of the lives and selected works by four leading Africana women writers —Global Prize-winning author Mariama Bâ (*So Long a Letter*), Nobel laureate Toni Morrison (*Beloved*), Popular Culture novelist Terry McMillan (*Disappearing Acts*), & twenty-first-century award-winning novelist Angie Thomas (*The Hate U Give*)—will be enhanced by careful readings of four theory books from the Africana Womanism Trilogy— *Africana Womanism: Reclaiming Ourselves*, 6th Edition; *Africana Womanist Literary Theory*; and *Africana-Melanated Womanism: In It Together*—as well as readings of scholarly selections by and about the various authors. We will be highlighting the prioritization of Race, Class, and Gender, a major cornerstone of this paradigm, committed to the empowerment and equality of all.

For Part I of the course, students will be introduced to the authentic Africana theoretical paradigm, Africana Womanism, and for Part II, they will be applying it to the four Africana womanist novels as they reflect our daily lives worldwide. Together, the primary and secondary reading materials, and other media materials, will enhance students' understanding of critical current issues, particularly as they relate to Africana women and their families and communities.

The ultimate objective of the course, then, is to enhance one's knowledge and appreciation of Africana women and their interconnection with their families (men and children) in particular, and Africana life and culture (historically and currently) in general. Its purpose is to introduce students to a relatable theoretical construct, as a possible antidote to some of the other female-based theories, such as various feminisms. Africana Womanism is an authentic Africana paradigm, designed specifically for all women of African descent, and by extension, for all men and women in general, as it demonstrates that we are, after all, IN IT TOGETHER!

Cultural Diversity Intensive Statement

The very foundation of the continuing emancipation framework, undergirding the Academic curriculum, though not originally accepted, predates today's diversity initiative in the Academy, introducing Black Studies to the Academy in the 60s. Thus, for the course, Africana Womanist Writers—20th &21st Centuries (4420/7420), students will be introduced to an authentic Africana theoretical concept, Africana Womanism, and they will be applying it to four Africana womanist novels. Together, all materials will enhance their understanding of critical current issues relevant to Africana women & their families/ communities. Utilizing Africana theoretical frameworks as a more workable analytical tool of analysis for Black life, the course prepares students for being better multi-dimensional, layered learners, who in turn will be able to bring this broader kind of understanding through a diverse global critical lens for all, thus transferring knowledge. Through enhancing learning, they will become more actively engaged in perhaps all disciplines for the ultimate benefit of all humanity. To achieve a better understanding of true Cultural Diversity, as advocated by the renowned twentieth-century scholar, Dr. W.E.B. Dubois, my goal as professor/scholar and, moreover, progenitor of Africana Womanism remains that of focusing on the student. In assisting them in enhancing their scope and knowledge, relative to the African American literary tradition, the utilization of Africana paradigms for authentic interpretations is, indeed, critical, in much the same way as we have come to understand the lives of others. Thus, the future for humanity can be better when we come to really know each other. In taking Diversity Intensive courses, then, students will be escalated to a better intellectual platform as transferers of knowledge, via a broader communicative basis, whereby we can experience a better worldview for all humanity.

Textbooks and Course Materials

Primary Sources (Required)

Bâ, Mariama—*So Long a Letter* (Waveland Press 2012)

Hudson (Weems), Clenora—*Africana-Melanated Womanism: In It Together* (Cambridge Scholars Publishing 2022)

——— *Africana Womanism: Reclaiming Ourselves*, Sixth Ed. (Routledge Press 2023; original 1993)

——— *Africana Womanist Literary Theory* (Africa World Press 2004)

McMillan, Terry—*Disappearing Acts* (Knopf 1989)

Morrison, Toni—*Beloved* (Alfred A. Knopf, 1987) Thomas, Angie—*The Hate U Give* (HarperCollins)

Secondary Sources (Selections from these Selections are required)
Samuels, Wilfred & Clenora Hudson (Weems). *Toni Morrison* (Prentice-Hall, 1990)
YouTube — "Africana Womanism: A Global Paradigm for Human Survival" Bowdoin College, 2015 https://www.youtube.com/watch?v=iUZ1gie-Uqk&t=304s
Handouts and Announcements, etc.—On Canvas
Grade Determination
3 + unexcused absences result in lowering class grade a minimum of 1 grade level.*
(If you anticipate barriers related to the format or requirements of this course, if you have emergency medical information, disabilities, etc. to share with me, please let me know as soon as possible.)
-- Class Participation—15%
-- Oral Report (10–15 minutes)—15%
-- Quizzes (2–3)—20%
-- Mid-Term—25%
-- Research Paper (7–10 pages)—25%

Weeks 1–15

1 *Student Introduction*—Name, Home, Classification, Major, Interest in Course; Expectations & Things you wish to contribute from your particular experiences or observations.

Course Overview—Course Requirements—Class Participation; Oral Reports; Quizzes; Mid-Term Exam; Research Paper (Proper Documentation), etc.

Details for **Oral Reports**—What is expected, i.e., Format & Content **Research Paper**—Follow **MLA** Style Sheet

All Selections—to be read before scheduled class period for discussion

2 **YouTube**— "Africana Womanism" (Bowdoin College, 2015)
Part I of *Africana Womanism: Reclaiming Ourselves*, Routledge Edition
Preliminary Materials: i.e., Endorsements; Forewords, Preface

3 Chapter I— "Africana Womanism"
Chapter 2— "Cultural & Agenda Conflicts in Academia"
Chapter 3— "Africana Womanism: A Theoretical Need"

4 Chapter 4—"The Agenda of the Africana Womanist"
Conclusion—*Africana Womanism*
Africana Womanist Literary Theory (AWLT)—Preliminaries

5 Chapter I—"*Nommo*—Self-Naming, Self-Definition"
Chapter III—"Africana Womanism: The Authentic Agenda"
Chapter IV—"Proud Africana Women Activists"

6 Chapter V—"Genuine Sisterhood or Lack Thereof"
Chapter VI —Africana Male-Female Relationships & Sexism"
Chapter X/Conclusion; Epilogue; Afterword

7 Chapter 11—"Authenticating & Validating Africana-Melanated Womanism: A Global Paradigm for Human Survival" (from *Africana Womanism*)
Chapter 12—"Africana Womanism's Race, Class and Gender: Pre-Intersectionality" (from *Africana Womanism*)

8 *Africana-Melanated Womanism: In It Together:* (Preliminaries)
Part I—Chapter 1—"The Significance of an Africana Womanism Paradigm: Collectivity & Interconnectedness for Social Justice" (Clenora Hudson (Weems)
Part II—Chapter 4—"Reclaiming Africana-Melanated Women: The Future of Africana Family/The Power of the Media" (Marquita M. Gammage)
Part III—Chapter 10—"Today's Civil/Human Rights Movements: Africana Men & Women Together—Against Racism & Emmett Till Continuums in a 5-Step Solution" (C. Hudson (Weems))

9 **Mid-Term Exam**
Prologue: 2000 interview with the author (*Africana Womanism*, xxi–xxxii)
Application of Theory to Text (Novels)—Part II of *Africana Womanism*
"Bâ's *So Long a Letter*: A Family Affair"—Chapter 6—(from *Africana Womanism*)

10 Toni Morrison
Quiz on *Beloved*
Samuels & Hudson (Weems)' *Toni Morrison*—Chapter 1—"As Big As Life"
ORAL REPORTS
Beloved: From Novel to Movie, Chapter IX (*Africana Womanist Literary Theory*)

11 "Morrison's *Beloved*: All Parts Equal," Chapter 8 (from *Africana Womanism*)
Samuels & Hudson (Weems)' *Toni Morrison*—Chapter 6—"Ripping the Veil: Meaning through Rememory in Beloved"
ORAL REPORTS

12 Terry McMillan's *Disappearing Acts*
Quiz—*Disappearing Acts*
ORAL REPORTS
"McMillan's *Disappearing Acts*: In it Together"—Chapter 9 (from *Africana Womanism*)

13 McMillan Cont.
Angie Thomas' *The Hate U Give*
Quiz
ORAL REPORTS

14 Thomas' *The Hate U Give*: Collectivity and Connectivity for Social Justice (from New Special Edition of *Africana Womanism*, Chapter 10)
ORAL REPORTS
Intense Discussion on Racial Dominance—Yesterday versus Today

15 **Course Wrap-Up**
Reflections; Discussion
Course Evaluations
Research Paper (7–10 pages)
Suggested Topics

a The applicability of Africana Womanism to Africana Women
b Africana Womanist Reading of Africana Womanist Novel(s)
c Africana Womanists Characters in Action in Literature
d Connectivity versus *Intersectionality*
e Collectivity/Connectivity for Ultimate Victory

***Africana Womanism: "I Got Your Back, Boo"* (Hudson—FEB 2009)**

Don't you know by now, girl, we're all In It Together.
Family-Centrality—that's it; we're going nowhere /out the other.
That means the men, the women, and children, too,
Truly collectively working—"I got your back, Boo."

***Racism* means the violation of our constitutional rights,**
Which creates on-going legal and even physical fights;
This 1st priority for humankind is doing what it must do,
Echoing our 1st lady, Michelle—"I got your back, Boo."

***Classism* is the hoarding of financial privileges,**
Privileges we must all have now in pursuit of happiness.
Without a piece of the financial pie, we're doomed to have a coup.
Remember—protect the other—"I got your back, Boo."

***Sexism*, the final abominable sin of female subjugation,**
A battle we must wage right now to restore our family relations.
All forms of sin inevitably fall under 1 of the 3 offenses.
A W—"I got your back, Boo"—corrects our common senses.

(Clenora Hudson, "Africana Womanism: 'I Got Your Back, Boo'" 2009)

Index

For Product Safety Concerns and Information please contact our EU representative GPSR@taylorandfrancis.com
Taylor & Francis Verlag GmbH, Kaufingerstraße 24, 80331 München, Germany

www.ingramcontent.com/pod-product-compliance
Lightning Source LLC
LaVergne TN
LVHW010932110826
845149LV00013B/2563

* 9 7 8 1 0 3 2 7 2 0 0 4 3 *